KWELLER PREP

COMMON CORE

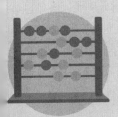

GRADE 5

MATHEMATICS

Kweller Prep

Developed by a lawyer, Kweller Prep is an established supplemental education service with a 15-year track record of success in preparing students for specialized middle-school, high-school, college entrance, and graduate school exams. With thousands of acceptances to date, Kweller Prep has built a time-tested learning program with unsurpassed performance. Our competitive advantage is the way in which we operate; we focus on each child individually to ensure success.

Our rigorous program is designed for ambitious students to help them achieve their academic goals. Tutoring centers in Queens and Manhattan serve as learning incubators where parents, students, teachers, tutors, and counselors alike can learn from one another and grow. Nearly every tutor at Kweller Prep is the first one in his or her family to attend a Specialized High School or Top University on a scholarship.

Kweller Prep was created by the vision of Frances Kweller, attorney at law. She was the first one in her immediate family to attend both a top university (New York University - Steinhardt School of Education) and Graduate Program (Juris Doctorate - Hofstra University School of Law). In short, Kweller Prep is designed to help get you where you want to go! 2 locations! Forest Hills, Queens and midtown Manhattan.

Email : info@kwellerprep.com

Website: **www.KwellerPrep.com**

First Edition January 2019.

This is the first edition so if you find any errors, please correct the error and then take a picture of the correction and the page number. Please email it to info@kwellerprep.com. Ms. Kweller will you $1 for any typo you find before May 1, 2019.

Copyright © 2019 by Origins Publications

Written by: Kweller Prep in collaboration with Origins Publications

All rights reserved. This book or any portion thereof may not be reproduced or used in any manner whatsoever without the express written permission of the publisher.

ISBN 13: 978-1-948255-70-7

The NY State Department of Education is not affiliated with Kweller Prep or Origins Publications and has not endorsed the contents of this book.

Origins Publications
New York, NY, USA
Email:info@originspublications.com

TABLE OF CONTENTS

Introduction 4
How To Use This Book 5
Test Prep Tips 6

Operations and Algebraic Thinking 7
Evaluate Numerical Expressions (5.OA.A.1) 8
Write & Interpret Numerical Expressions (5.OA.A.2) 12
Use Numerical Patterns & Graph Ordered Pairs in Coordinate Plane (5.OA.B.3) ... 15

Number and Operations In Base Ten 20
Understand Place Value (5.NBT.A.1) 21
Powers of 10 (5.NBT.A.2) 24
Read, Write and Compare Decimals (5.NBT.A.3) 27
Rounding Decimals (5.NBT.A.4) 30
Multiply Multi-digit Whole Numbers (5.NBT.B.5) 33
Divide Whole Numbers (5.NBT.B.6) 36
Add, Subtract, Multiply & Divide Decimals (5.NBT.B.7) 39

Number and Operations-Fractions 42
Add and Subtract Fractions (5.NF.A.1) 43
Solve Word Problems Involving Subtraction & Addition of Fractions (5.NF.A.2) 47
Divide Whole Numbers and Fractions (5.NF.B.3) 51
Multiply Whole Numbers and Fractions (5.NF.B.4) 55
Interpret Multiplication as Scaling (5.NF.B.5, 5.NF.B.5.A, 5.NF.B.5.B) 59
Solve Word Problems Involving Multiplication of Fractions (5.NF.B.6) 63
Solve Word Problems Involving Division of Fractions
(5.NF.B.7, 5.NF.B.7.A, 5.NF.B.7.B, 5.NF.B.7.C) 66

Measurement and Data 70
Convert Units of Measurement (5.MD.A.1) 71
Display Data in Line Plots & Solve Problems Using Line Plots (5.MD.A.2) 74
Recognize & Understand Volume (5.MD.C.3) 78
Measure Volume by Counting Cubes (5.MD.C.4) 82
Solve Problems Involving Volume (5.MD.C.5) 87

Geometry 92
Understand Graph Points on the Coordinate Plane (5.G.A.1) 93
Solve Problems Using Coordinate Plane (5.G.A.2) 96
Understand Attributes of Two-Dimensional Shapes (5.G.B.3) 100
Classify Two-Dimensional Shapes (5.G.B.4) 104

Answer Key and Explanations 109

Practice Tests 128
Practice Test One & Answer Key Explanations 129
Practice Test Two & Answer Key Explanations 153

INTRODUCTION

Common Core Standards / Next Generation Learning Standards

States all across the USA have implemented rigorous standards called the "Common Core Standards." These standards, or learning goals, outline what students in each grade should learn each year. They emphasize just how important the new goals are: they can help show whether students are on the right track to college and beyond, even when the students are years from those life stages.

In 2018, NY introduced the "Next Generation Learning Standards", which are very similar to the Common Core standards in that they focus on higher level critical thinking skills, problem solving, analysis, and real-world application.

NY State Mathematics Assessments

The NY State math assessment is designed to determine whether students have mastered grade level appropriate mathematics skills.

The assessment is given annually in grades 3-8, and is administered in either computer-based or paper-based formats.

The test is divided into two sessions that are administered over two days. Session 1 consists of multiple-choice questions. Session 2 consists of multiple choice, short-response, and extended-response questions. Students will NOT be permitted to use calculators in Grades 3–5.

Students will be provided as much time as necessary to complete each test session.

Students in Grade 5 will likely need approximately 80–90 minutes to complete Session 1 and 70–80 minutes to complete Session 2.

Question Format on NY State Math Assessments

The tests contain multiple-choice, short-response, and extended-response questions.

For **multiple-choice questions**, students select the correct response from four answer choices.

For **short- and extended-response questions**, students write an answer to an open ended question and may be required to show their work. In some cases, they may be required to explain, in words, how they arrived at their answers.

Extended-response questions allow students to show their understanding of mathematical procedures, conceptual understanding, and application. They may also assess student reasoning and the ability to critique the arguments of others.

HOW TO USE THIS BOOK

The objective of this book is to provide students, educators, and parents with practice materials focused on the core skills needed to help students succeed on the NY State mathematics assessment.

A student will fare better on an assessment when s/he has practiced and mastered the skills measured by the test. A student also excels when s/he is familiar with the format and structure of the test. This book helps students do both. Students can review key material by standard through doing the skill-building exercises, as well as take practice tests to become accustomed to how the content is presented and to enhance test-taking skills. By test day, students will feel confident and be adequately prepared to do his or her best.

This Book Includes:

- 348 skill-building exercises organised by standard in order to help students learn and review concepts in the order that they will likely be presented in the classroom. These worksheets also help identify weaknesses, and highlight and strengthen the skills needed to excel on the actual exam. A variety of question formats are included in the worksheets to help students build skills in answering different questions types and to engage students' interest as they work through problems.

- Our mathematics practice tests are based on the official NYS mathematics assessments released by the test administrator. Our practice tests include similar question types and the same rigorous content found on the official assessments. By using these materials, students will become familiar with the types of items (including TEIs presented in a paper based format) and response formats they may see on the test. Two practice tests are included at the end of the book.

- Answer keys with detailed explanations to help students not make the same mistakes again. These explanations help clear up common misconceptions and indicate how students might arrive at an answer to a question.

- The answer explanations for the practice tests also identify the standard/s that the question is assessing. If a student is having difficulty in one area, encourage the student to improve in that area by practicing the specific set of skills in the workbook.

- Test prep tips to help students approach the test strategically and with confidence.

TEST PREP TIPS

First of all, remind your student to pay attention in class throughout the year, asking questions as needed on homework and classwork. The curriculum should follow the exact standards and skills that will be tested on the end-of-year assessment.

Another extremely effective strategy is to practice, practice, practice. Have your student work on practice questions and complete several full length practice tests. Our practice tests are a great place to start.

However, simply answering the questions and then moving on will not yield much improvement. If your student misses a question, discuss why the correct answer is indeed correct. Come up with alternate approaches to this question type that may work better in the future. Have your student explain his or her answer to each question. This gives you the opportunity to reinforce logical thinking and correct misconceptions as needed.

Prior to the test, ensure that your student has a solid night of sleep and eats a nourishing breakfast.

For children, avoiding test anxiety is very important, so be sure to avoid over-emphasizing the test or inadvertently causing your student to feel excessive stress or pressure.

In addition, teach your student general test-taking strategies such as the following:

Use your "Work Folder" (if provided with one) to write out problems, create charts and graphs, or draw pictures and diagrams as necessary. This portion is not graded, so do whatever you think will help you visualize and correctly solve the problem.

If you get stuck on a question, skip it and come back to it after answering easier questions.

There is no penalty for incorrect answers, so answer every question, even if you ultimately have to guess. On multiple choice questions, a 25% chance of answering correctly is still much better than no chance.

Don't panic when you get stuck on a question. Take a deep breath and remember that you are intelligent and prepared. No one is expected to answer every single question correctly.

If you follow the tips here, your student should be well on her way to a stress-free and successful performance on this important assessment.

OPERATIONS AND ALGEBRAIC THINKING

 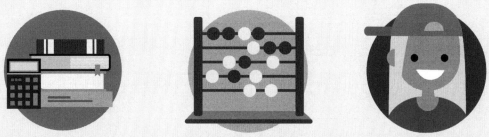 

EVALUATE NUMERICAL EXPRESSIONS

5.OA.A.1 Use parentheses, brackets, or braces in numerical expressions, and evaluate expressions with these symbols.

1. In this equation, which part must be completed first?

    $$[(5 + 3) \times 15] - 4 \times 4 = n$$

    A. 3 x 15
    B. 5 + 3
    C. 4 x 4
    D. 8 – 4

2. In this equation, which part must be completed second?

    $$55 \times \{2 + [85 - (21 + 2)]\} = n$$

    A. 21 + 2
    B. 2 + 62
    C. 85 - 23
    D. 82 - 21

3. What is the third step in completing this equation?

    $$7 \times 2 - 4 + (12 - 3 \times 3) = n$$

    A. 7 x 2
    B. 3 x 3
    C. 12 - 3
    D. 4 + 3

4. What is the value of the expression below?

    $$(9 \times 2 - 4) - 20 \div 5 =$$

    A. 14
    B. 12
    C. 16
    D. 10

5. What is the last step in this equation?

    31 + (14 – 2 x 3) x 2

    A. 31 x 2
    B. 31 + 16
    C. 36 x 2
    D. 39 x 2

6. Carson bought a jumbo pack of gum with 36 sticks of gum. He keeps 6 sticks of gum for himself and shares the rest between 5 friends. Which expression can be used to find how many sticks of gum each friend receives?

    A. (36 – 6) ÷ 5
    B. (36 ÷ 6) - 5
    C. 36 ÷ 6 - 5
    D. 36 – (6 + 5)

7. What is the value of the expression below?

    3 x {[6 + 10 - (7 + 3) - 2] + 5}

    A. 30
    B. 24
    C. 27
    D. 39

8. Which expression shows the next step needed to solve:

    30 + 8 ÷ 2 – (10 + 2)

    A. 38 ÷ 2 – (10 + 2)
    B. 30 + 6 – (10 +2)
    C. 38 ÷ 2 - 12
    D. 30 + 8 ÷ 2 - 12

9. Every morning for a week Maggie bikes 5 miles in the morning and 8 miles in the afternoon. How many miles does Maggie bike? Which expression can be used to solve?

    A. 5 x 7 +8
    B. 7 x (5 + 8)
    C. (5 + 8) x 5
    D. (5 x 8) x 7

OPERATIONS & ALGEBRAIC THINKING

10. Explain how to solve this expression step-by-step:

$$24 + \{[3 + (8 \times 2) - 6] \times 2\}$$

① 8×2   ② 3+16−6   ③ 24+[13×2]

11. Use the table to solve parts A and B below

1. 3 × (5 + 6)	**A.** Marshall has $6 and spent $3 on a smoothie. Then he found $5 in his car.
2. (3 × 5) + 6	**B.** Mary reads 5 pages of her book after breakfast and 6 pages after dinner for 3 days.
3. 5 + (6 − 3)	**C.** Bryant bought 3 bags of candy for $5 each and a toy for $6.

Part A. Match the expressions to the word problems. Write the letter of the word problem to match the equation on the line.

1. B
2. C
3. A

Part B. Evaluate each expression:

1. 33
2. 21
3. 8

12. Use the chart below to solve part A and B. There is no sales tax at the School Store.

School Store	
Item	Cost
Notebook	$5
Pack of Markers	$4
Ruler	$2
Binder	$3

Part A. Harry has $20 to spend at the school store. He buys 2 binders and 1 ruler and 2 packs of markers. Write an expression to find how much money Harry will have left over after purchasing these items.

20 − x

Part B. Does Harry now have enough money to purchase a notebook? Explain

Part C. How many markers, rulers **or** binders can Harry purchase with the change he received from the first purchase?

WRITE & INTERPRET NUMERICAL EXPRESSIONS

5.OA.A.2 Write simple expressions that record calculations with numbers, and interpret numerical expressions without evaluating them. *For example, express the calculation "add 8 and 7, then multiply by 2" as 2 × (8 + 7). Recognize that 3 × (18932 + 921) is three times as large as 18932 + 921, without having to calculate the indicated sum or product.*

---

1. Which expression matches the phrase "16 added to 3 times as much as 2"?
    - **A.** (3 x 3) + 16
    - **B.** (3 x 2) + 16
    - **C.** (2 + 3) + 16
    - **D.** (16 + 3) x 2

2. Which phrase describes the expression:

    4 x (321 + 190)

    - **A.** 4 times three-hundred twenty-one plus one hundred ninety
    - **B.** 4 times the difference of three-hundred twenty-one and one hundred ninety
    - **C.** 4 times as much as the sum of three-hundred twenty-one and one hundred ninety
    - **D.** 4 times as much as three-hundred twenty-one

3. Which expression matches the phrase "30 thirty-twos minus 1 thirty-two"?
    - **A.** 30 + 32 + 32
    - **B.** 30 + 32 - 32
    - **C.** 30 x 32 + 32
    - **D.** 30 x 32 - 32

4. Jerry bought 8 packs of baseball cards. 7 packs had 21 cards and one pack had 15 cards. Which expression shows Jerry's total number of baseball cards?
    - **A.** 15 + (7 x 21)
    - **B.** (7 + 21) + 15
    - **C.** (8 x 21) + 15
    - **D.** 15 + (7 + 8)

5. Sherry bought 4 trays of 12 cupcakes for a party. The cupcakes were shared between 16 people. Which expression shows how many cupcakes each person received?
    - **A.** (4 + 12) ÷ 16
    - **B.** (4 x 12) - 16
    - **C.** 4 x 12 + 16
    - **D.** (4 x 12) ÷ 16

OPERATIONS & ALGEBRAIC THINKING

6. Mark has 45 stickers. He gave his 8 friends 5 stickers each. Which expression can be used to find how many stickers Mark has left?
   A. (45 − 8) × 5
   B. 45 − (8 × 5) ✓
   C. 45 − (8 + 5)
   D. (45 − 8) ÷ 5

7. Cara is reading a 180-page book. The first day she reads 40 pages, and she then reads equal amounts for the next 7 days. Which expression can be used to find how many pages Cara needs to read each day?
   A. (180 − 40) - 7
   B. 180 − (40 ÷ 7)
   C. (180 − 40) ÷ 7
   D. (180 + 40) - 7

8. Marco made 7 trays with 6 cookies in each tray. He kept 10 cookies for himself and gave 4 cookies to each of his friends. Which expression can be used to find the number friends Marco shared with?
   A. [(7 × 6) − 10] ÷ 4
   B. [(7 × 6) + 10] ÷ 4
   C. (7 × 6) − (10 ÷ 4)
   D. [(7 × 6) ÷ 10] × 4

9. The cost of renting a private room for an event at a restaurant is $80 and to feed each person costs $30. Which expression can be used to find c, the cost in dollars of the private room rental and number of people, n, eating at the event?
   A. $c = 80n + 30$
   B. $c = 30(n + 80)$
   C. $c = 80 \times 30n$
   D. $c = 30n + 80$

10. Compare the expressions using >, <, =.

    3 seventeens, tripled   4 times the sum of 18 and 29

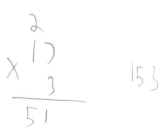

OPERATIONS & ALGEBRAIC THINKING

11. Lylah has $25. She bought 4 sandwiches for $5.50 each and a bag of chips for $1.95. What equation can be used to find how much change, c, Lylah received?
(No sales tax added)

   Part A. What is the first step in solving this problem? _____

   Part B. Will Lylah be able to purchase a cookie for $1.50? Why or why not?

   _____

   _____

   _____

   _____

12. Wilson works 8 hours a week and makes $12 an hour. He saves his money for 3 weeks and then purchases a new video game console for $150, how much money will he have left?

   Part A. Write an expression to solve this problem: _____

   Part B. Solve the expression: _____

USE NUMERICAL PATTERNS & GRAPH ORDERED PAIRS IN COORDINATE PLANE

5.OA.B.3 Generate two numerical patterns using two given rules. Identify apparent relationships between corresponding terms. Form ordered pairs consisting of corresponding terms from the two patterns, and graph the ordered pairs on a coordinate plane. *For example, given the rule "Add 3" and the starting number 0, and given the rule "Add 6" and the starting number 0, generate terms in the resulting sequences, and observe that the terms in one sequence are twice the corresponding terms in the other sequence. Explain informally why this is so.*

1. The table shows a set of number pairs.

X	Y
2	5
5	8
6	9

If the points are plotted on a coordinate grid, which of the following ordered pairs would be on the gird?
   A. (1, 3)
   B. (3, 5)
   C. (5, 8)
   D. (2, 4)

2. A set of points are plotted on a coordinate grid: (1, 3) (3, 5) (4, 6). If all the ordered pairs follow the same pattern, which ordered pair would be on the coordinate grid?
   A. (8, 10)
   B. (7, 10)
   C. (5, 8)
   D. (6, 9)

3. What is the next set of number in this pattern?
   x: 2, 6, 10, 14, 18
   y: 5, 11, 17, 23, 29

   A. (23, 35)
   B. (22, 36)
   C. (22, 35)
   D. (24, 36)

4. The pattern below starts at 2 and uses the rule "Add 3".

   2, 5, 8, 11, 14, 17

   A second pattern starts at 3 and uses the rule "Add 2". What is the difference between the 6th term in first pattern and 6th term in the second pattern?
   - A. 3
   - B. 5
   - C. 6
   - **D. 4** ✓

   (work shown: 17 − 13 = 4; 3, 5, 7, 9, 11, 13)

5. Sue writes a number pattern that starts at 27 and subtracts 3 as the rule. John writes a number pattern that starts at 32 and subtracts 4 as the rule. What is the fifth term in both patterns?
   - **A. (15, 16)** ✓
   - B. (18, 20)
   - C. (16, 18)
   - D. (19, 21)

   (work shown: 27, 24, 21, 18, 15; 32, 28, 24, 20, 16)

6. The table shows the total cost of renting a car for a different number of hours.

Number of Hours (n)	Cost of Rental Car in dollars (d)
2	30
4	60
6	90
8	120

   Which equation can be used to find the total cost in dollar, *d*, of renting a car for a certain number of hours, *n*?
   - A. $d = n + 28$
   - **B. $d = n \times 15$** ✓
   - C. $d = n \times 20$
   - D. $d = 18 \times n$

7. There are two patterns shown below:

    Pattern A: 3, 6, 9, 12, 15
    Pattern B: 6, 12, 18, 24, 30

    What is the relationship between the patterns?
    A. Pattern A is double Pattern B
    B. Pattern B is three times as much as Pattern A
    C. Pattern B is two times as much as Pattern A
    D. Pattern A is one third of pattern B

8. The graph below shows a line segment with 3 points on the coordinate grid. What is the last ordered pair needed to complete the grid?

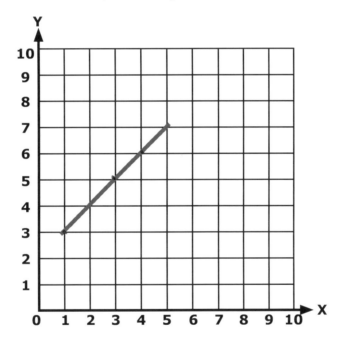

Coordinate Grid

x	1	3	
y	3	5	

A. (5, 7)
B. (5, 8)
C. (7, 5)
D. (6, 7)

9. Kaitlin has a cup of tea that is 160°F. She adds 3 ice cubes and the temperature drops 12° every 8 minutes. What is the temperature of the water after 24 minutes?

   A. 132
   B. 136
   C. 148
   D. 124 ← (circled)

10. The table below shows the cost of ordering pizzas for catering a party.

Number of Pizzas (p)	Total Cost (c) (dollars)
3	$12
6	$24
8	$32
10	$40

Part A. Write an equation that describes the relationship between the number of pizzas (*p*) and the total cost (*c*).

_____

Part B. Use the equation to find out how much 15 pizzas would cost. _____

11. Benjamin and Luke work at the bike shop and start saving their money. Benjamin saves $3 per day and Luke save $9 per day. Complete the table to show Benjamin's and Luke's total savings at the end of the day for the first 5 days.

Day	1	2	3	4	5
Benjamin's Savings					
Luke's Savings					

What is the relationship between Benjamin's savings amount and Luke's savings amount?

_____

_____

_____

12. Complete the tables given the patterns. Then use the points to plot the lines on the coordinate grid.

$y = 3x$ $y = 2x + 1$

x	y
1	
2	
3	
4	

x	y
1	
2	
3	
4	

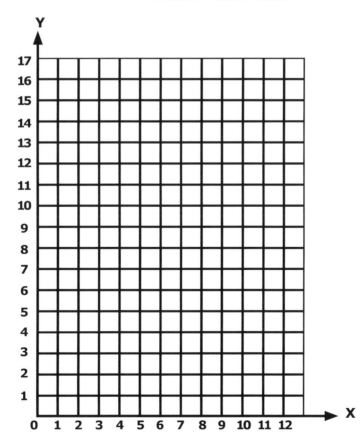

NUMBER AND OPERATIONS IN BASE TEN

UNDERSTAND PLACE VALUE

5.NBT.A.1 Recognize that in a multi-digit number, a digit in one place represents 10 times as much as it represents in the place to its right and $1/10$ of what it represents in the place to its left.

1. Choose the correct answer to fill in the blank:
   Ten times as much as 100 is _____
   - A. 10
   - B. 100
   - **C. 1,000**
   - D. 10,000

2. Choose the correct answer to fill in the blank:
   Ten times as much as _____ is 40,000
   - A. 40
   - **B. 4,000**
   - C. 400
   - D. 410

3. Choose the correct answer to fill in the blank:
   One hundred times as much as 1,360 is _____
   - A. 13,600
   - B. 130,600
   - C. 1,360,000
   - **D. 136,000**

4. What place value is one-tenth of the thousands place value?
   - **A. hundreds**
   - B. ten thousands
   - C. tens
   - D. hundred thousands

5. What is $1/100$ of 1.2?
   - A. 0.12
   - **B. 0.012**
   - C. 1.200
   - D. 120

6. Jenna has $1/10$ the amount of LEGOs as Tommy. Tommy has 430 LEGOs. How many LEGOs does Jenna have?

   A. 4,300
   B. 403
   C. 43
   D. 4.3

7. A microscope is set to enlarge objects 100 times as large as their original size. Juan looks at a fly that is 0.072 cm long. How long will the fly appear through the microscope?

   A. 72 cm
   B. 720 cm
   C. 0.72 cm
   D. 7.2 cm

8. The distance on a map from the coffee shop to the pharmacy is 0.529 yards. The actual distance is one thousand times as large. What is the actual distance from the coffee shop to the pharmacy?

   A. 529 yards
   B. 52.90 yards
   C. 5,290 yards
   D. 52,900 yards

9. About one-tenth of 12 million people have dogs. How many people have dogs?

   A. 120 thousand
   B. 1.2 million
   C. 120 million
   D. 12 thousands

10. Compare the place value of the 5 in 152,378 to the place value of the 5 in 24,589 using the place value system.

_____

_____

_____

_____

_____

11. Use the numbers 6,245.39 and 364.5 to solve A-D.

Part A. Which number has the digit 3 in a smaller place value?_____

Part B. What is the value of the 3 in 6,245.39? _____

Part C. What is the value of the 3 in 364.5? _____

Part D. How many times smaller is it? Explain using place value

_____

_____

_____

12. Carl thinks 30 hundredths is the same as 3 thousandths because 30 hundreds equals 3 thousands. Is Carl correct or incorrect? Use place value to explain.

_____

_____

_____

What is another way to write 30 hundredths? _____

POWERS OF 10

5.NBT.A.2 Explain patterns in the number of zeros of the product when multiplying a number by powers of 10, and explain patterns in the placement of the decimal point when a decimal is multiplied or divided by a power of 10. Use whole-number exponents to denote powers of 10.

1. What is the value of 10^4?
   - A. 100
   - B. 1,000
   - **C. 10,000** ✓
   - D. 100,000

   10000

2. What is the value of 2.34×10^3?
   - A. 23.4
   - B. 0.234
   - C. 234
   - **D. 2,340** ✓

   2.34 × 1,000 = 2,340

3. What is the value of $542.8 \div 10^2$?
   - A. 5.428
   - B. 54.28
   - C. 0.5428
   - D. 5,428

4. What is 100 x 1,000 written in exponential form?
   - A. 10^3
   - B. 10^4
   - C. 10^5
   - D. 10^2

5. What is $145,000 \div 10^6$ in standard form?
   - A. 14.5
   - B. 0.145
   - C. 145
   - D. 0.0145

6. Based on the pattern, which number completes this sequence?

    8,700,000   87,000   _____   8.7

    A. 8,700
    B. 870
    C. 87
    D. 0.87

7. Kara solved her math problem by moving the decimal point 3 places to the right as shown.

    3.687 → 3,687

    Which of the descriptions explains how Kara got her answer?
    A. She divided 3.687 by 10
    B. She multiplied 3.687 by 100
    C. She divided 3.687 by 1,000
    D. She multiplied 3.687 by 1,000

8. What is this number in standard form?

    $(4 \times 10^3) + (0.5 \times 10^2) + (35 \times \frac{1}{100}) + (6 \times \frac{1}{1000})$

    A. 4,050.356
    B. 4,503.56
    C. 405.356
    D. 45.356

9. The table below shows a set of numbers.

Number	Number ÷ 100
356.24	3.5624
283	2.83
1,397.6	13.976

    Which pair of numbers could be added to the table? Select ALL that apply.
    ☐ 43.81 and 4.381
    ☐ 923.9 and 9.239
    ☐ 65.7 and 0.657
    ☐ 104.78 and 1,047.8
    ☐ 100.14 and 10.14

10. Samuel thinks 10^5 is the same as 500,000.

   A. Is he correct? Explain your reasoning using place value.

   _____

   _____

   _____

   _____

   B. What is the value of 10^5? _____

11. Mr. Holmes writes 2.45×10^3 is the same as $245,000 \div 10^2$.

   A. Write each number in standard form and them compare them.
   B. Is he correct? Explain your reasoning.

   _____

   _____

   _____

   _____

12. Solve 456×10^3 and $456 \div 10^3$.

   $456 \times 10^3 =$ _____

   $456 \div 10^3 =$ _____

   C. Explain why the numbers are different.

   _____

   _____

   _____

READ, WRITE AND COMPARE DECIMALS

5.NBT.A.3 Read, write, and compare decimals to thousandths.

1. Which phrase is the correct wording for this decimal?

    14.507

    A. fourteen five hundred seventy
    B. fourteen and five hundred seven thousandths
    C. fourteen and fifty-seven hundredths
    D. fourteen five hundred thousandths

2. Which decimal represents this decimal in standard form?

    three and twenty-six thousandths

    A. 3.26
    B. 30.26
    C. 3.026
    D. 3.206

3. Which decimal has a 4 in the hundredths place?

    A. 4.406
    B. 0.084
    C. 8.134
    D. 25.54

4. Which decimal is shown by point A on the number line below?

    A. 1.4
    B. 1.04
    C. 14
    D. 0.4

5. Which set of decimals below is correctly compared?
   A. 3.56 < 3.54
   B. 45.67 > 45.63
   C. 0.45 < 0.4
   D. 1.07 > 1.09

6. What is this number in standard form?

   $$(4 \times 100) + (5 \times 1) + (9 \times 1/10) + (4 \times 1/1000)$$

   A. 450.94
   B. 450.904
   C. 405.094
   D. 405.904

7. Which decimal below is the largest?
   A. sixty-four and 5 hundredths
   B. $(6 \times 10) + (5 \times 1/10) + (8 \times 1/100)$
   C. $(6 \times 10) + (4 \times 1) + (5 \times 1/10) + (8 \times 1/100)$
   D. 64.058

8. Which decimal below is the smallest?
   A. $2.8 \div 10^3$
   B. $2.8 \div 100$
   C. $2.8 \times 1/10$
   D. $2.8 \times 1/100$

9. Which decimals are ordered from least to greatest?
   A. 67.90, 67.09, 67.99
   B. 3.478, 3,48, 3.5
   C. 9.081, 9.018, 0.8
   D. 145.33, 145.3, 145.34

10. Compare the decimals below by using >, < or =.

    4 and 5 tenths _____ 0.45

    9.322 _____ 09.232

    0.6 _____ 6 x $\frac{1}{100}$

    0.038 _____ $\frac{38}{100}$

11. Use the decimal 94.532 so solve parts A and B.

    Part A. Write 94.532 in expanded form using fractions.

    _____

    Part B. Write 94.532 in word form.

    _____

    _____

12. Use the decimal 56.7 to solve parts A, B, and C.

    Part A. Solve: 56.7 ÷ 100 = _____

    Part B. Solve 56.7 x $\frac{1}{100}$ = _____

    Part C. Explain what happens to a decimal when you divide by 100 and multiplying by $\frac{1}{100}$.

    _____

    _____

    _____

ROUNDING DECIMALS

5.NBT.A.4 Use place value understanding to round decimals to any place.

1. Use the number line to round 13.7 to the nearest ones place.

   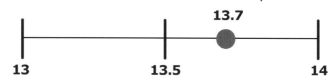

   A. 13.5
   B. 14
   C. 13
   D. 13.7

2. Use the number line to round 6.43 to the nearest tenths place.

   A. 6.4
   B. 6.5
   C. 7
   D. 6

3. Round 873.5 to the nearest whole number.
   A. 870
   B. 873
   C. 872
   D. 874

4. Round 14.472 to the nearest hundredths place.
   A. 14.48
   B. 14.4
   C. 14.47
   D. 14.5

5. Which decimal below would be rounded to 23.6?
   A. 23.57
   B. 23.54
   C. 23.69
   D. 23.66

6. Sarah uses 0.997 cups of butter to make cookies. What is this number rounded to the nearest hundredths place?
   A. 0.99
   B. 1.0
   C. 0.97
   D. 0.98

7. Which of the numbers below is rounded to 490.73
   A. 490.736
   B. 409.731
   C. 490.70
   D. 490.732

8. Round 134.8348 to the nearest thousandths place.
   A. 134.834
   B. 134.830
   C. 134.835
   D. 134.836

9. Which pair of decimals correctly rounds 72.54 to two different place values?
   A. 72.5 and 73.0
   B. 72.55 and 73.0
   C. 73.0 and 72.0
   D. 72.53 and 70.0

10. Round 3.561 to the:
    A. nearest hundredths place _____
    B. nearest tenths place _____
    C. nearest ones place _____

11. What is the largest and smallest decimal written to the hundredths place that could be rounded to 56.3?

   A. Largest decimal: _____

   B. Smallest decimal: _____

12. One quart is equal to 0.946 liters. Josh rounds this amount to 0.95 liters and Sandra rounds this amount to 0.9. Who is correct? Explain your reasoning.

MULTIPLY MULTI-DIGIT WHOLE NUMBERS

5.NBT.B.5 Fluently multiply multi-digit whole numbers using the standard algorithm.

1. What is the product of 6,300 x 30?
    - **A.** 18,900
    - **B.** 189,000
    - **C.** 18,090
    - **D.** 1,890,000

2. What is product of 42 tens x 4 hundreds?
    - **A.** 16,800
    - **B.** 1,680,00
    - **C.** 168,000
    - **D.** 16,808

3. What is the product of 451 x 28?
    - **A.** 12,628
    - **B.** 4,150
    - **C.** 12,228
    - **D.** 11,628

4. A baby hippo weighs 90 pounds. It will grow to be 42 times its weight as an adult hippo. How much will the adult hippo weigh?
    - **A.** 3,680 pounds
    - **B.** 3,780 pounds
    - **C.** 378 pounds
    - **D.** 3,880 pounds

5. Carter pays $129 each month for his cell phone bill. How much money his cell phone cost him for a year?
    - **A.** $1,538
    - **B.** $387
    - **C.** $1,548
    - **D.** $1,558

6. Which expression is not equivalent to 64 x 38?
   - **A.** 64 x (37 + 1)
   - **B.** (64 x 30) + (64 x 8)
   - **C.** 64 groups of 38
   - **D.** (60 x 30) + (4 x 8)

7. A football stadium sells 12,425 tickets for each home game. If the team plays 23 games at home this season, how many tickets will the stadium sell?
   - **A.** 285,775 tickets
   - **B.** 285,725 tickets
   - **C.** 275,775 tickets
   - **D.** 245,735 tickets

8. Southern School District purchases 350 new laptops. Each laptop costs $789. How much money does the school district spend on new laptops?
   - **A.** $276,160
   - **B.** $276,150
   - **C.** $276,180
   - **D.** $266,150

9. Marsha saves $145 a week. Janet saves $58 more a week than Marsha. How much money did Janet save for 35 weeks?
   - **A.** $5,075
   - **B.** $7,205
   - **C.** $7,105
   - **D.** $7,055

10. Carlos saves $125 a month. He saves $45 less than James. How much money will James save in 1.5 years?

11. Jill walks 3 dogs a day and gets paid $20 for each dog. If she walks the same 3 dogs for 168 days, how much money will Jill make?

_____

_____

If Jill decides to walk 5 dogs at the same rate for 45 days, how much money will she make total?

_____

_____

12. The 5th grade class goes on a field trip to the museum. There are 25 adults and 112 students on the trip. Each adult ticket costs $14 and each student ticket costs $9. How much will it cost for the adults and students to enter the museum?

Solve: _____

_____

A special exhibit at the museum costs an extra $12 for everyone. What is the total cost of the regular tickets and the special exhibit tickets for everyone on the trip?

_____

_____

DIVIDE WHOLE NUMBERS

5.NBT.B.6 Find whole-number quotients of whole numbers with up to four-digit dividends and two-digit divisors, using strategies based on place value, the properties of operations, and/or the relationship between multiplication and division. Illustrate and explain the calculation by using equations, rectangular arrays, and/or area models.

1. Which division equation does this area model show?

	400	+	50	+	7
3					

   A. 475 ÷ 3 =
   B. 450 x 3 =
   C. 457 ÷ 3 =
   D. 450 ÷ 3 =

2. Which equation could help you solve 3,465 ÷ 25?
   A. 3,465 x 25 = n
   B. 25 x n = 3,465
   C. 3,465 − 25 = n
   D. 3,465 + 25 = n

3. Solve 35,000 ÷ 700 =
   A. 500
   B. 5,000
   C. 5
   D. 50

4. A concert arena holds 45,000 people. There are 5,000 seats in each section. How many sections are in the concert arena?
   A. 9
   B. 90
   C. 900
   D. 9,000

5. The area of a gymnasium is 864 square feet. If the width of the gym is 27 feet, what is the length of the gym? Choose the equation needed to solve this problem.
    A. 864 x 27 =
    B. 864 + 27 =
    C. 864 ÷ 27 =
    D. 864 − 27 =

6. How many groups of twenty-four are in forty-eight hundred?
    A. 2
    B. 200
    C. 2,000
    D. 20

7. Caden organizes buttons into containers at the sewing store. She divides 568 buttons into groups of 32. How many containers will she need to organize all the buttons?
    A. 17 containers
    B. 24 containers
    C. 41 containers
    D. 18 containers

8. Samantha shares 85 cupcakes with her 13 classmates and herself. She gives the leftover cupcakes to her teacher. How many cupcakes will her teacher receive?
    A. 1 cupcake
    B. 6 cupcakes
    C. 7 cupcakes
    D. 2 cupcakes

9. Middletown High School is having a bake sale. The students made 2,568 cookies that were split into a dozen cookies per box. Each box sold for $14. How much money did the school make on the bake sale if they sold every box of cookies? Which equation can be used to solve this problem?
    A. (2,568 x12) ÷ 14 =
    B. 2,568 - (12 x 14) =
    C. (2,568 ÷12) x 14 =
    D. 2,568 ÷ (12 x 14) =

10. A number divided by 36 has a quotient of 16 with a remainder of 5. What is the number? Show your work.

   Part A. Answer: _____

   Part B. Write the division equation for this problem: _____

   Part C. Write the multiplication equation for this problem: _____

11. Thomas divided 3,280 by 16 and his answer was 200 remainder 80. Explain his error. Then correctly solve the problem.

   Part A. Explain Thomas' error:

   _____

   _____

   _____

   Part B. Solve the problem:

12. Carline drives 25 minutes to the store. It takes her 3 minutes to walk into the store from the parking lot. If Carline spent 5 hours and 36 minutes traveling to the store and back in one month, how many round trip visits to the store does Caroline take to the store each month?

_____

_____

ADD, SUBTRACT, MULTIPLY & DIVIDE DECIMALS

5.NBT.B.7 Add, subtract, multiply, and divide decimals to hundredths, using concrete models or drawings and strategies based on place value, properties of operations, and/or the relationship between addition and subtraction; relate the strategy to a written method and explain the reasoning used.

1. Choose the correct answer.

$$45.6 \times 10^4 =$$

   A. 45,600
   B. 456,000
   C. 4,560
   D. 4,560,000

2. Choose the correct answer.

$$87.23 \div 10^3 =$$

   A. 0.08723
   B. 8.723
   C. 0.8723
   D. 8,723

3. The model below shows a decimal multiplication problem. Choose the equation that represents this model.

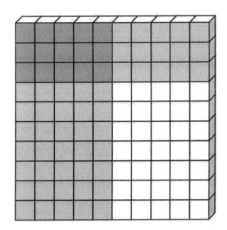

   A. 0.3 x 0.5 = 1.5
   B. 0.3 x 0.5 = 15
   C. 0.3 x 0.5 = 0.015
   D. 0.3 x 0.5 = 0.15

NUMBER AND OPERATIONS IN BASE TEN

4. Camille bought a sweater for $15.95 and a scarf for $8.75. If she pays with $30, how much change should she receive (no tax added)?
    A. $5.70
    B. $6.20
    C. $5.30
    D. $6.70

5. Cecee is shopping for bakery items. She buys 4 bags of flour for $6.69 each and 3 bags of chocolate chips for $3.55. How much money does Cecee spend at the supermarket?
    A. $36.50
    B. $37.31
    C. $37.41
    D. $36.31

6. The population of Kelly's hometown is 40,000 people. The population of Tommy's hometown is $^2/_{10}$ of the population of Kelly's town. What is the population of Tommy's hometown? Which equation is needed to solve this problem?
    A. 0.2 ÷ 40,000 =
    B. 40,000 ÷ 0.2 =
    C. 40,000 x 0.10
    D. 40,000 x 0.2 =

7. Mrs. Jones has 0.8 of a birthday cake leftover from her party to share with her friends the next day. If she splits the cake into 0.2 size pieces, how many friends can Mrs. Jones share with?
    A. 0.8 ÷ 0.2 = 4
    B. 0.8 x 0.2 = 0.16
    C. 0.2 ÷ 0.8 = 0.25
    D. 0.8 ÷ 0.2 = 0.4

8. Which of the following statements is true about the product of a decimal times a decimal. Example: 0.5 x 0.56
    A. The product is always greater than 1.
    B. The product is between the two factors.
    C. The product is less than the two factors.
    D. The product is greater than the two factors.

9. Explain why a tenth times a tenth equals a number in the hundredths using pictures, equations, or models.

_____

_____

_____

_____

10. Joel is building a garden bed. He makes the width of the garden 5.4 feet. He wants the length to be 1.4 times as long as the width.

   Part A. What is the length of the garden?

   _____

   Part B. If Joel wants to make a second garden that is half the area of the first garden, what is the area of the second garden?

   _____

11. Shreya hikes 5.8 miles on Saturday with an average speed of 2 and a half miles per hour. How long will it take her to complete the hike on Saturday?

   Part A. Show your work and explain your answer.

   _____

   _____

   Part B. On Sunday, Shreya hiked the same amount but at a faster pace of 2.9 miles per hour. How many hours did Shreya hike on Saturday and Sunday.

   _____

   _____

NUMBER & OPERATIONS – FRACTIONS

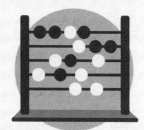

ADD AND SUBTRACT FRACTIONS

5.NF.A.1 Add and subtract fractions with unlike denominators (including mixed numbers) by replacing given fractions with equivalent fractions in such a way as to produce an equivalent sum or difference of fractions with like denominators. *For example, $2/3 + 5/4 = 8/12 + 15/12 = 23/12$. (In general, $a/b + c/d = (ad + bc)/bd$.)*

---

1. Which bar model represents the sum of $2/8 + 1/4$?

   A.

   B.

   C.

   D.

2. What is the sum of $1/3 + 1/6$?

   A. $2/3$ C. $3/6$

   B. $2/6$ D. $4/6$

3. What is the least common denominator for $1/5$ and $1/6$?
   A. 30
   B. 35
   C. 20
   D. 25

NUMBER & OPERATIONS – FRACTIONS

4. What are the equivalent fractions that can be used to solve $\frac{3}{4} + \frac{2}{6}$?

   A. $\frac{12}{24} + \frac{10}{24}$

   B. $\frac{5}{6} + \frac{2}{6}$

   C. $\frac{12}{18} + \frac{4}{18}$

   D. $\frac{9}{12} + \frac{4}{12}$

5. What is the least common denominator of $\frac{3}{4}$, $\frac{3}{8}$, and $\frac{3}{20}$?

   A. 40

   B. 30

   C. 20

   D. 60

6. Callie is baking a cake. She uses $2\frac{2}{3}$ cups of flour and $1\frac{1}{4}$ cups of sugar. How many more cups of flour and sugar did Callie use to make the cake?

   A. $1\frac{11}{12}$ cups

   B. $3\frac{11}{12}$ cups

   C. $1\frac{5}{12}$ cups

   D. $1\frac{4}{12}$ cups

7. Juan needs $1\frac{4}{5}$ ounces of chocolate to bake a dessert. He has $1\frac{3}{7}$ ounces in the pantry. How many more ounces of chocolate does he need?

   A. $\frac{23}{35}$ ounces

   B. $\frac{13}{35}$ ounces

   C. $1\frac{13}{35}$ ounces

   D. $1\frac{3}{25}$ ounces

8. Johnson drives to his grandparents' house and uses $\frac{3}{8}$ of a gallon of gas. The next day he uses $\frac{1}{3}$ of a gallon of gas to the store and $\frac{4}{6}$ of a gallon to drive back home. How many gallons of gas did Johnson use?

   A. $1\frac{13}{24}$ gallons

   B. $2\frac{8}{24}$ gallons

   C. $1\frac{11}{24}$ gallons

   D. $1\frac{9}{24}$ gallons

9. Nola has a 1 pound box of pasta. She cooks $\frac{1}{2}$ pound on Monday, $\frac{2}{5}$ pound on Tuesday. How much pasta does Nola have left to cook on Wednesday?

    A. $\frac{1}{10}$ pound

    B. $\frac{2}{10}$ pound

    C. $\frac{9}{10}$ pound

    D. $\frac{4}{10}$ pound

10. Amber planted flowers in $\frac{3}{4}$ of a flowerbed. Katie planted some flowers too. Together, they planted flowers in $1\frac{9}{10}$ of a flowerbed. What fraction of the flowerbed did Katie plant?

Explain your answer:

_____

_____

_____

11. Jackie has 5 cups of sugar. She uses $1\frac{4}{5}$ cup to make cookies and $2\frac{1}{4}$ cup to make a cake. Then she uses $\frac{2}{10}$ cup for bread. How much sugar does Jackie have left?

    Part A. What is the first step needed to solve?

_____

_____

_____

    Part B. How much sugar does Jackie have left? Simplify your answer.

_____

_____

_____

NUMBER & OPERATIONS – FRACTIONS

12. Frank went to the store with $5. He spent $1\,1/6$ of his dollars on a sandwich, $3/8$ of the dollars on a granola bar and $1\,3/4$ of his dollars on a pizza. What fraction of his dollars does Frank have left?

Part A. What is the first step needed to solve?

Part B. What fraction of his dollars does Frank have left? Simplify your answer.

SOLVE WORD PROBLEMS INVOLVING SUBTRACTION & ADDITION OF FRACTIONS

5.NF.A.2 Solve word problems involving addition and subtraction of fractions referring to the same whole, including cases of unlike denominators, e.g., by using visual fraction models or equations to represent the problem. Use benchmark fractions and number sense of fractions to estimate mentally and assess the reasonableness of answers. For example, recognize an incorrect result $2/5 + 1/2 = 3/7$, by observing that $3/7 < 1/2$.

1. Use the number line to add $2\,1/4$ and $1\,1/2$. What is the sum?

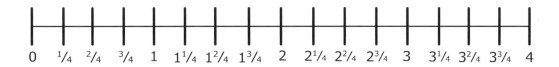

   A. $3\,1/4$

   B. $3\,1/2$

   C. $3\,3/4$

   D. 4

2. Kevin eats $3/8$ of a chocolate bar on Tuesday and $1/5$ of the same chocolate bar on Wednesday. About what fraction of the chocolate bar did Kevin eat?

   A. $1/2$　　C. $4/5$

   B. $1/4$　　D. $7/8$

3. Emily drinks $5/6$ pint of orange juice and $2/5$ pint of milk for breakfast. About how many more pints of orange juice than milk did Emily drink? Choose the equation to solve this problem.

   A. $1/2 + 1 =$

   B. $1 - 1/4 =$

   C. $1/2 - 1/2 =$

   D. $1 - 1/2 =$

NUMBER & OPERATIONS – FRACTIONS

4. Samuel bought $2/3$ gallon of soda and $3/5$ gallon of iced tea for a party. How many gallons of drinks did Samuel buy?

    A. $1\ 4/15$ gallons

    B. $1\ 5/15$ gallons

    C. $1\ 9/15$ gallons

    D. $1\ 6/15$ gallons

5. Justin spends $1\ 1/6$ hour washing his car and $4/5$ hour vacuuming his car. About how many hours does Justin spend cleaning his car?

    A. 1 hour 15 minutes

    B. 2 hours

    C. 1 hour

    D. 3 hours

6. Ryan is building a bench. He uses $3\ 7/8$ feet of maple timber and $2\ 2/6$ feet of walnut timber. How many more feet of maple timber did Ryan use?

    A. $12/24$ feet

    B. $1\ 5/8$ feet

    C. $1\ 13/24$ feet

    D. $1\ 1/2$ feet

7. Leo used $1/3$ of his allowance to buy a new game. Then he used $3/7$ of his allowance to buy a new toy. What fraction of the allowance does Leo have left?

    A. $7/21$

    B. $16/21$

    C. $15/21$

    D. $5/21$

8. Stephanie baked apple pie. She gave $1/8$ to her friend Shelly, $1/4$ to her friend Tom, and she ate $2/12$ of the pie. How much of the pie remains?

    A. $11/24$

    B. $13/24$

    C. $10/24$

    D. $10/12$

9. Jill has 5 $\frac{1}{7}$ feet of red wrapping paper and 3 $\frac{7}{8}$ feet of blue wrapping paper, and 4 $\frac{3}{6}$ feet of pink wrapping paper. About how many feet of wrapping paper does Jill have?

   A. 12 feet

   B. 15 feet

   C. 13 $\frac{1}{2}$ feet

   D. 11 feet

10. Karen is estimating how much flour she needs if each cake requires 2 $\frac{2}{6}$ cups of flour and she is making 3 cakes.

    Explain how many cakes Karen can make:

    _____
    _____
    _____
    _____
    _____
    _____

11. It takes Kelly $\frac{4}{6}$ of an hour to get to school. It takes Mason $\frac{5}{8}$ of an hour to get to school. It takes Joey $\frac{10}{12}$ of an hour to get to school.

    A. Who spends the most time getting to school? _____

    B. How much time does it take Mason and Kelly to get to school? _____

    C. Simplify your answer: _____

NUMBER & OPERATIONS – FRACTIONS

12. Rashid is counting the leftovers from his party. He has $1\frac{1}{6}$ of a vegetable pizza, $\frac{1}{10}$ of a pepperoni pizza and $\frac{2}{5}$ of a plain pizza left.

   Part A. How much pizza is left? Simplify your answer.

   _____

   _____

   Part B. How much more of the vegetable pizza is left than the plain pizza?

   _____

   _____

DIVIDE WHOLE NUMBERS AND FRACTIONS

5.NF.B.3 Interpret a fraction as division of the numerator by the denominator ($a/b = a \div b$). Solve word problems involving division of whole numbers leading to answers in the form of fractions or mixed numbers, e.g., by using visual fraction models or equations to represent the problem. *For example, interpret $3/4$ as the result of dividing 3 by 4, noting that $3/4$ multiplied by 4 equals 3, and that when 3 wholes are shared equally among 4 people each person has a share of size $3/4$. If 9 people want to share a 50-pound sack of rice equally by weight, how many pounds of rice should each person get? Between what two whole numbers does your answer lie?*

---

1. Which model shows $1 \div 4$ or 1 out of 4 shaded?

    A.
    B.
    C.
    D.

2. Which fraction shows this division equation?

$$1 \div 6$$

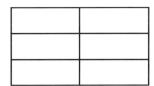

   A. $2/5$
   B. $1/6$
   C. $2/6$
   D. $1/5$

NUMBER & OPERATIONS – FRACTIONS

3. The fraction $^2/_3$ can be written as which division equation?

   A. $3 \div 3 =$
   B. $3 \div 2 =$
   C. $2 \div 2 =$
   D. $2 \div 3 =$

4. Josh draws a model to show $2 \div 5$ because he has 2 pizzas to share with 5 friends. Which fraction represents what part of a pizza each person will receive?

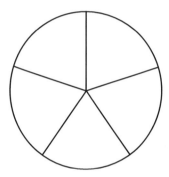 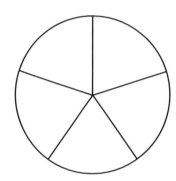

   A. $^2/_5$
   B. $^5/_2$
   C. $^5/_5$
   D. $^1/_5$

5. Carly, Mary, and Joan share 4 sandwiches. How many parts of the sandwich does each friend receive? Use the diagram to help you choose the correct answer.

 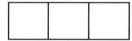  

   A. $3 \div 4 = ^3/_4$
   B. $3 \div 4 = ^3/_3$
   C. $4 \div 3 = 1\ ^1/_3$
   D. $4 \div 3 = 1\ ^3/_4$

6. Jack is dividing 5 bags of dog food between 6 dogs. Which equation shows how Jack should divide the food equally?

A. 5 ÷ 5 = 1

B. 6 ÷ 5 = $^6/_5$

C. 5 ÷ 6 = 1 $^5/_6$

D. 5 ÷ 6 = $^5/_6$

7. John, Matt, and Carlos share the yard work. Their yard is 14 feet long and they divide the yard evenly. Which equation shows how the boys should divide up the yard work?

A. 14 ÷ 3 = 4

B. 14 ÷ 3 = 4 $^2/_3$

C. 3 ÷ 14 = 4 $^2/_2$

D. 3 ÷ 14 = $^3/_{14}$

8. Maggie is cutting up ribbon for a craft project. She has 4 feet of ribbon that she needs to cut into 8 pieces. How long should each piece of ribbon be?

A. $^1/_2$ foot

B. $^8/_4$ foot

C. 2 feet

D. 1 $^1/_2$ feet

9. Carrie and her 5 friends are volunteering to organize the food pantry. They will sort and organize 4 boxes of food. How much will each girl have to organize?

A. $^4/_5$ of a box

B. $^6/_4$ of a box

C. $^2/_3$ of a box

D. $^1/_2$ of a box

NUMBER & OPERATIONS – FRACTIONS

10. 8 friends are sharing a 42-pound bag of coffee. How much coffee will each get?

   Part A. The answer is between which 2 whole numbers? _____

   Part B. What is the exact answer? _____

11. 6 friends share 2 pizzas equally.

   Part A. Draw a picture to represent the 2 pizzas and how they should be shared with 6 people.

   Part B. How much of the pizza will each person receive? _____

12. Main Street bakery uses 3 cups of flour to make 6 mini cakes.

   Part A. How many cups of flower are in each mini cake? Show your work:

   _____

   Part B. 3 friends came into the bakery and bough the 6 mini cakes. How many cakes will each friend get? Show your work:

MULTIPLY WHOLE NUMBERS AND FRACTIONS

5.NF.B.4 Apply and extend previous understandings of multiplication to multiply a fraction or whole number by a fraction.

5.NF.B.4.A Interpret the product *(a/b) × q* as a parts of a partition of q into b equal parts; equivalently, as the result of a sequence of operations *a × q ÷ b*. For example, use a visual fraction model to show *(2/3) × 4 = 8/3*, and create a story context for this equation. Do the same with *(2/3) × (4/5) = 8/15*. *(In general, (a/b) × (c/d) = (ac)/(bd)).*

5.NF.B.4.B Find the area of a rectangle with fractional side lengths by tiling it with unit squares of the appropriate unit fraction side lengths, and show that the area is the same as would be found by multiplying the side lengths. Multiply fractional side lengths to find areas of rectangles, and represent fraction products as rectangular areas.

1. Use the model below to help you solve $\frac{1}{3}$ x 3.

   A. $\frac{1}{3}$

   B. 3

   C. $\frac{2}{3}$

   D. $\frac{3}{3}$

2. Which equation shows $\frac{1}{4} + \frac{1}{4} + \frac{1}{4} + \frac{1}{4} + \frac{1}{4}$?

   A. $\frac{1}{4}$ x 5 =

   B. $\frac{1}{4}$ + 5 =

   C. $\frac{1}{4}$ x 4 =

   D. $\frac{1}{4}$ + 4 =

3. Which equation shows one way to solve 4 x $\frac{2}{5}$?

   A. $\frac{2}{5} + \frac{2}{5} + \frac{2}{5} =$

   B. $\frac{2}{5} + \frac{2}{5} + \frac{2}{5} + \frac{2}{5} =$

   C. $\frac{4}{5} + \frac{4}{5} + \frac{4}{5} + \frac{4}{5} =$

   D. $\frac{2}{5} + \frac{2}{5} + \frac{2}{5} + \frac{2}{5} + \frac{2}{5} =$

NUMBER & OPERATIONS – FRACTIONS

4. Colton is counting the leftovers from his party. There are 3 pizzas with $^1/_6$ of each pizza remaining. How much pizza is remaining?

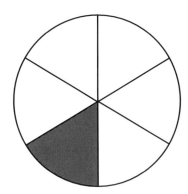
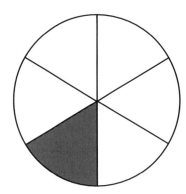
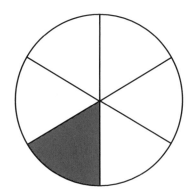

A. $^3/_3$

B. $^1/_9$

C. $^3/_6$

D. $^1/_6$

5. Patrick is learning how to multiply fractions and rewrites 5 x $^4/_7$ to show the first step when multiplying. Which could be his answer?

A. $\dfrac{4}{7 \times 5}$

B. $\dfrac{5 \times 4}{7}$

C. $\dfrac{4 + 5}{7}$

D. $\dfrac{4}{5 + 7}$

6. Sherry has $^6/_8$ of a cake leftover from her birthday. Of the leftover cake, $^1/_3$ of it has icing. What fraction of the leftover cake has icing?

A. $^6/_8$ x $^1/_3$ = $^6/_{24}$

B. $^6/_8$ + $^1/_3$ = $^7/_{11}$

C. $^6/_8$ - $^1/_3$ = $^5/_5$

D. $^6/_8$ x $^1/_3$ = $^6/_{11}$

7. Use the shaded model to help you solve $3/4 \times 4/5$?

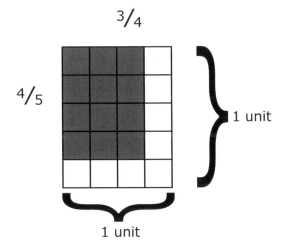

A. $12/4$

B. $7/9$

C. 12

D. $12/20$

8. Bianca is planting flowers in her garden bed that is $7/8$ yard long by $5/8$ yard wide. What is the area of the flowerbed? Use the model below to help you solve.

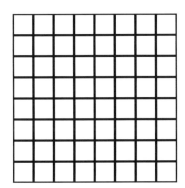

A. $7/8 + 5/8 = 12/8$

B. $7/8 - 5/8 = 2/8$

C. $7/8 \times 5/8 = 35/64$

D. $7/8 \div 5/8 = 56/40$

9. In Mrs. Kelly's 5th grade math class, $2/3$ of the students have pets. Of those students with pets, $3/4$ of them have dogs. What fraction of all the students have dogs? Select the answer in simplest form.

   A. $5/6$

   B. $1/2$

   C. $1/3$

   D. $6/10$

10. James scored $4/20$ of the points in his basketball game. The team scored 80 points during the game. How many points did James score?

    Part A. Write the equation needed to solve this problem: _____

    Part B. Solve and explain your answer:

11. Hadley says if she multiplies a fraction by the number 4, the resulting product will be less than 4. Is she correct? Use an example or model to explain your thinking.

12. Michael needs to find the area of the canvas he is painting. The length of the canvas measures $4/5$ foot and the width is $4/6$ foot. Draw a model to show how you can represent this problem. Then solve.

    Model:

    Answer in simplest form: _____

INTERPRET MULTIPLICATION AS SCALING

5 NF.B.5 Interpret multiplication as scaling (resizing), by:

5 NF.B.5.A Comparing the size of a product to the size of one factor on the basis of the size of the other factor, without performing the indicated multiplication.

5 NF.B.5.B Explaining why multiplying a given number by a fraction greater than 1 results in a product greater than the given number (recognizing multiplication by whole numbers greater than 1 as a familiar case); explaining why multiplying a given number by a fraction less than 1 results in a product smaller than the given number; and relating the principle of fraction equivalence a/b = (n × a)/(n × b) to the effect of multiplying a/b by 1

1. Which equation shows how 4 was scaled up to 12 on the number line?

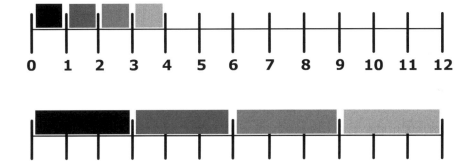

   A. 4 + 3 = 12

   B. 3 x 4 = 12

   C. 12 - 3 = 4

   D. 12 - 4 = 3

2. Which equation shows how 3 was scaled up to 12 on the number line?

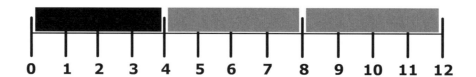

A. 4 + 3 = 12

B. 3 x 3 = 12

C. 4 x 3 = 12

D. 12 − 4 = 3

3. Use the number line to find $^1/_4$ scaled up 5 times.

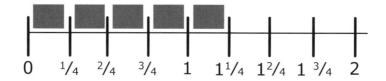

A. $^1/_4$ x 5 = $^5/_4$

B. $^1/_4$ x 5 = $^4/_4$

C. $^1/_4$ + 5 = $^5/_4$

D. $^1/_4$ + 5 = $^6/_4$

4. What is the product of 6 x $^2/_3$? Choose the answer that describes the comparison of the product to the factor 6. Use the number line to help you solve.

A. $^2/_3$ x 6 > 6
B. $^2/_3$ x 6 = 6
C. 6 > $^2/_3$ x 6
D. $^2/_3$ x 6 < 6

5. Use the number line to find 1 ½ scaled up 3 times.

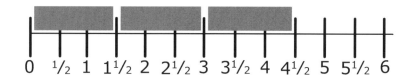

   A. 1 ½ x 3 = 4
   B. 1 ½ x 3 = 4 ½
   C. 1 ½ x 3 = 4 ¼
   D. 3 - 1 ½ = 2 ½

6. Which statement is true about 13 x ⁸/₈ ?
   A. The product will be less than 13.
   B. The product will be greater than 13.
   C. The product will be equal to 13.
   D. The product will 2 times more than 13.

7. Which statement is true about 4 x ²/₅ ?
   A. The product will be less than 4.
   B. The product will be greater than 4.
   C. The product will be equal to 4.
   D. The product will less than zero.

8. Which statement is true about 1 ⁴/₈ x 5 ?
   A. The product will be less than 5.
   B. The product will be greater than 5.
   C. The product will be equal to 5.
   D. The product will less than zero.

9. Choose the equation that will have the largest product without solving.
   A. ½ x ⁵/₆
   B. ⅓ x ³/₃
   C. ⁷/₈ x 5
   D. 3 x 2 ¾

NUMBER & OPERATIONS – FRACTIONS

10. Robert thinks that multiplying a whole number by a fraction will always results in a product that is smaller than the whole number. Is he correct? Explain why or why not with models or pictures.

_____
_____
_____

11. Choose a single fraction to complete each inequality correctly.

   Part A. ³/₄ x _____ > ³/₄

   Part B. 6 x _____ < 6

   Part C. ⁶/₄ x _____ < ⁶/₄

   Part D. Then explain how you know your answers are correct by choosing one problem to explain.

_____
_____
_____

12. Complete the expression with <, >, = without multiplying.

   2 ⁴/₅ x ¹/₃ _____ 2 ⁴/₅

Explain why the product of 2 ⁴/₅ x ¹/₃ is more, less than, or equal to 2 ⁴/₅.

_____
_____
_____

SOLVE WORD PROBLEMS INVOLVING MULTIPLICATION OF FRACTIONS

5.NF.B.6 Solve real world problems involving multiplication of fractions and mixed numbers, e.g., by using visual fraction models or equations to represent the problem.

---

1. There are 25 students in Mrs. Jones' 5th grade class. $2/5$ of the students are boys. How many boys are in Mrs. Jones' class? Choose the equation needed to solve.
    - **A.** $25 - 2/5 =$
    - **B.** $25 + 2/5 =$
    - **C.** $25 \times 2/5 =$
    - **D.** $25 \div 2/5 =$

2. Sam's Theater sold 112 movie tickets on Saturday. $3/4$ of the tickets sold were adult tickets. How many adult tickets were sold?
    - **A.** 84 adult tickets
    - **B.** 79 adult tickets
    - **C.** 28 adult tickets
    - **D.** 90 adult tickets

3. Addison walks her dog $9/12$ of a mile. On her walk, she decides to jog for $1/6$ of the time. What fraction of the miles is spent running? Choose the equation needed to solve.
    - **A.** $9/12 + 1/6 =$
    - **B.** $9/12 - 1/6 =$
    - **C.** $9/12 \div 1/6 =$
    - **D.** $9/12 \times 1/6 =$

4. Amanda's painting is $3/4$ foot long. How long is her painting in inches?
    - **A.** 8 inches
    - **B.** 9 inches
    - **C.** 6 inches
    - **D.** 10 inches

5. Caroline painted $6/8$ of her painting blue. Then she added stars to $4/5$ of the blue part of her painting. What fraction of the painting has stars? Simplify your answer.
    - **A.** $3/5$ of the painting
    - **B.** $2/6$ of the painting
    - **C.** $1/2$ of the painting
    - **D.** $1/3$ of the painting

6. Mia has 48 ounces of chocolate. She uses $^5/_8$ of the chocolate for cookies and the rest to make brownies. How many ounces of chocolate does Mia use to make brownies?
    - **A.** 20 ounces
    - **B.** 18 ounces
    - **C.** 28 ounces
    - **D.** 30 ounces

7. Kevin scored 30 points during his basketball game. His teammates scored $^2/_3$ of the points during the game. How many points did his teammates score?
    - **A.** 30 points
    - **B.** 90 points
    - **C.** 45 points
    - **D.** 60 points

8. It took Jenna $^5/_6$ hour to drive to her grandmother's house. How long will it take Jenna to drive to her grandmother's house and back?
    - **A.** 1 hour
    - **B.** 1 hour 20 minutes
    - **C.** 1 hour 40 minutes
    - **D.** 1 hour 30 minutes

9. It took the Carol Family 8 $^2/_6$ hours to drive to Florida. $^2/_5$ of that time was spent eating lunch and taking a shopping break. How long did the Carol family spend on their lunch and shopping break?
    - **A.** 3 $^1/_3$ hours
    - **B.** 3 hours
    - **C.** 3 $^1/_5$ hours
    - **D.** 3 $^1/_6$ hours

10. Caleb ordered 4 $^1/_2$ pizzas. If $^3/_4$ of the pizzas were pepperoni pizzas, how many pizzas were pepperoni pizzas? Show your work:

Answer:_____

64   NUMBER & OPERATIONS – FRACTIONS

11. Steven and Corey share a 20-ounce bag of pretzels. Steven ate $^2/_5$ of the bag and Corey ate $^3/_{10}$ of the bag. How many ounces are left?

   Part A. What is the first step needed to solve this problem? _____

   Part B. How many ounces did the boys eat together? _____

   Part C. How many ounces of the pretzel bag are left? _____

12. Nathan, Anthony, and Charlie each have a 24-ounce water bottle filled with water. Nathan drank $^1/_3$ of his water, Charlie drank $^3/_8$ of his water and Anthony drank $^5/_6$ of his water.

   Part A. How many more ounces of water did Anthony drink than Charlie?

   _____

   Part B. How many ounces of water does Nathan have in his water bottle?

   _____

   Part C. How many ounces of water remain in all 3 water bottles?

   _____

SOLVE WORD PROBLEMS INVOLVING DIVISION OF FRACTIONS

5.NF.B.7 Apply and extend previous understandings of division to divide unit fractions by whole numbers and whole numbers by unit fractions.

5.NF.B.7.A Interpret division of a unit fraction by a non-zero whole number, and compute such quotients. *For example, create a story context for ($1/3$) ÷ 4, and use a visual fraction model to show the quotient. Use the relationship between multiplication and division to explain that ($1/3$) ÷ 4 = $1/12$ because ($1/12$) × 4 = $1/3$.*

5.NF.B.7.B Interpret division of a whole number by a unit fraction, and compute such quotients. *For example, create a story context for 4 ÷ ($1/5$), and use a visual fraction model to show the quotient. Use the relationship between multiplication and division to explain that 4 ÷ ($1/5$) = 20 because 20 × ($1/5$) = 4.*

5.NF.B.7.C Solve real world problems involving division of unit fractions by non-zero whole numbers and division of whole numbers by unit fractions, e.g., by using visual fraction models and equations to represent the problem. *For example, how much chocolate will each person get if 3 people share $1/2$ lb of chocolate equally? How many $1/3$-cup servings are in 2 cups of raisins?*

---

1. Harriet has 2 pizzas. If she cuts the pizzas into $1/3$ sized pieces, how many pieces of pizza will she have? Use the model below to help you solve.

   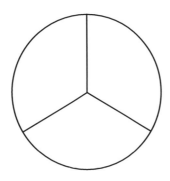 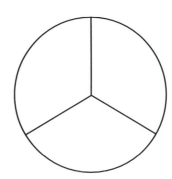

   A. 2 ÷ $1/3$ = 3 pieces

   B. 2 ÷ $1/3$ = 6 pieces

   C. 2 × $1/3$ = $2/3$ pieces

   D. 2 + $1/3$ = 1 $1/3$ pieces

2. Robbie has 4 feet of wood. He needs to cut it into $1/4$ foot pieces. How many pieces will Robbie have after cutting the wood? Use the model to help you solve.

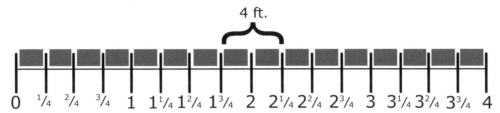

A. 16 pieces
B. 12 pieces
C. 10 pieces
D. 20 pieces

3. Mrs. Baker is making 3 cakes. How many pieces of cake will she have if she cuts each cake into $1/6$ sized pieces?

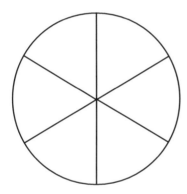 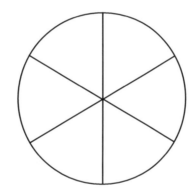 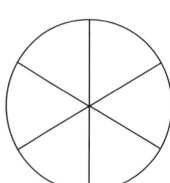

A. $3 \times 1/6 = 3/6$
B. $3 + 1/6 = 1\,4/6$
C. $3 \div 1/6 = 12$
D. $3 \div 1/6 = 18$

4. For an art project, Colby is dividing pieces of paper into fifths. How many fifth-sized pieces can Colby cut out of 6 pieces of paper?

A. 15 pieces
B. 20 pieces
C. 30 pieces
D. 35 pieces

NUMBER & OPERATIONS – FRACTIONS

5. 3 cups of water fills up $1/4$ of Jerry's bucket. How many total cups of water does Jerry's bucket hold?

   A. $3 \times 4 = 12$ cups

   B. $3 \times 1/4 = 3/4$ cups

   C. $3 + 1/4 = 2\,1/4$ cups

   D. $3 - 1/4 = 2$ cups

6. Hannah has $1/3$ of a brownie tray leftover. She shares the leftovers with 2 friends. What fraction of the brownie tray will each friend get to eat? Use the model to help you solve.

   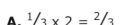

   A. $1/3 \times 2 = 2/3$

   B. $1/3 \div 2 = 1/6$

   C. $1/3 \div 2 = 6$

   D. $1/3 \times 2 = 1/6$

7. Brendan has $1/2$ pound of almonds to divide up into 8 snack bags. How many pounds of almonds did Brendan use to make each snack bag?

   A. $1/8$ pound

   B. $1/4$ pound

   C. $1/16$ pound

   D. $1/12$ pound

8. Kellen spent $5/6$ of his birthday money and put the remaining amount into 2 secret piggy banks. What fraction of his birthday money does Kellen put into each of the piggy banks?

   A. $1/10$ of the money

   B. $1/6$ of the money

   C. $1/8$ of the money

   D. $1/12$ of the money

9. Emma spends half of her day on Saturday cleaning the house. If she cleans 5 rooms, each for the same amount of time, what fraction of her day is spent cleaning each room?

   A. $1/10$ of her day

   B. $1/7$ of her day

   C. $1/20$ of her day

   D. $1/3$ of her day

10. Mrs. Smith bought 4 cakes for her son's birthday party. She wants each guest to have one-fourth of the cake. Draw picture to show many guests she can share the cake with.

Answer:_____

11. A recipe for an apple cake needs $^1/_3$ cup of oil, $^1/_2$ cup of apples, and $^1/_4$ cup of milk. If Samantha has 2 cups of oil, 4 cups of apples, and 3 cups of milk, how many cakes will each ingredient make?

    Part A. The amount of cakes made from the oil: _____

    Part B. The amount of cakes made from the apples: _____

    Part C. The amount of cake made from the milk:_____

    Part D. With all the ingredients Samantha has, how many cakes can she make? _____

12. Sandra has a pitcher of orange juice. She pours $^1/_6$ of the orange juice into 3 glasses.

    Part A. What fraction of the orange juice is in each glass? _____

    Part B. Sandra pours $^1/_3$ of the orange juice for herself and then pours the remaining orange juice into 4 smaller glasses. What fraction of the orange juice did she pour in each of the smaller glasses? _____

MEASUREMENT AND DATA

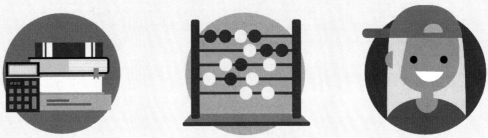

CONVERT UNITS OF MEASUREMENT

5.MD.A.1 Convert among different-sized standard measurement units within a given measurement system (e.g., convert 5 cm to 0.05 m), and use these conversions in solving multi-step, real world problems.

1. Kurt's textbook is 25 centimeters long. What is the length of the textbook in millimeters?
   - **A.** 0.25 millimeters
   - **B.** 250 millimeters
   - **C.** 2.5 millimeters
   - **D.** 25 millimeters

2. Mary's pet gerbil is $1/3$ of a foot long. How many inches long is the gerbil?
   - **A.** 6 inches
   - **B.** 3 inches
   - **C.** 5 inches
   - **D.** 4 inches

3. Cal spent $2/3$ of an hour working on his car. How many minutes did Cal spend working on his car?
   - **A.** 40 minutes
   - **B.** 30 minutes
   - **C.** 45 minutes
   - **D.** 20 minutes

4. The apple tree is 4.56 meters tall. What is the height of the tree in centimeters?
   - **A.** 45.6 centimeters
   - **B.** 4,560 centimeters
   - **C.** 456 centimeters
   - **D.** 45 centimeters

5. Jessie has a teapot with $1/5$ liters of tea. He pours the tea into 4 cups. How many milliliters are in each cup?
   - **A.** 50 milliliters
   - **B.** 500 milliliters
   - **C.** 40 milliliters
   - **D.** 200 milliliters

MEASUREMENT AND DATA

6. Margaret uses 2 pounds of cherries to make a 4 cherry tarts. How many ounces of cherries are in each tart?

    A. 10 ounces

    B. 8 ounces

    C. 12 ounces

    D. 16 ounces

7. Halidon has half a bottle of soda with 24 ounces. How many cups are in the *entire* bottle of soda?

    A. 5 cups

    B. 3 cups

    C. 8 cups

    D. 6 cups

8. Sally has 5 yards of rope. She cuts the rope into 6 equal pieces. How long is each piece of rope in inches?

    A. 36 inches

    B. 30 inches

    C. 32 inches

    D. 25 inches

9. 5 tigers weigh $1/2$ of a ton. How much does each tiger weigh in pounds?

    A. 200 pounds

    B. 500 pounds

    C. 600 pounds

    D. 300 pounds

10. The length of a bike is 168 centimeters.

    Part A. What is the length of the bike in meters? _____

    Part B. What is the length of the bike in millimeters? _____

11. Monica bought $7/8$ pound of grapes and $1/4$ pound of blueberries.

    Part A. How many ounces of grapes did Monica buy? _____

    Part B. How many ounces of blueberries did Monica buy? _____

    Part C. Monica bought 1 $1/2$ pounds of strawberries. Did she buy more ounces of grapes or strawberries? _____

12. Mason is painting the garage and fence outside. He needs 20 extra quarts of paint for the garage and splits the rest evenly. If he uses 220 quarts total, how many gallons of paint will he use for the fence?

    Show your work:

    Answer:_____

DISPLAY DATA IN LINE PLOTS & SOLVE PROBLEMS USING LINE PLOTS

5.MD.B.2 Make a line plot to display a data set of measurements in fractions of a unit ($\frac{1}{2}$, $\frac{1}{4}$, $\frac{1}{8}$). Use operations on fractions for this grade to solve problems involving information presented in line plots. *For example, given different measurements of liquid in identical beakers, find the amount of liquid each beaker would contain if the total amount in all the beakers were redistributed equally.*

Use the following line plot to answer questions 1-3.

The line plot shows the amount of rainfall for 2 weeks in October in inches.

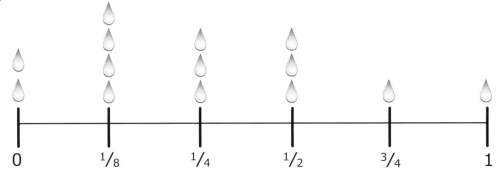

2 week rainfall — October (inches)

1. What was the most frequent amount of rainfall?

    A. $\frac{1}{4}$

    B. $\frac{1}{8}$

    C. $\frac{1}{2}$

    D. $\frac{3}{4}$

2. According to the line plot, how many days did it not rain?

    A. 2

    B. 3

    C. 4

    D. 0

3. What is the total amount of rainfall for the 2 weeks recorded in October?

    A. 4 inches

    B. 4 $\frac{1}{4}$ inches

    C. 4 $\frac{1}{8}$ inches

    D. 4 $\frac{1}{2}$ inches

Use the line plot to answer questions 4-6.

The line plot below shows the lengths of different pieces of ribbon in Jamie's craft drawer.

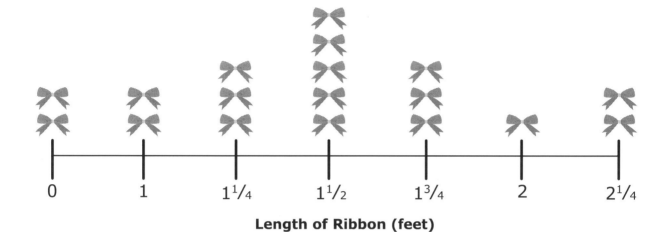

Length of Ribbon (feet)

4. What was the longest length of the ribbon?

    A. 1 1/2 ft.

    B. 3 ft.

    C. 2 1/4 ft.

    D. 2 ft.

5. What is the mode of the ribbons?

    A. 1 1/4 ft.

    B. 1 1/2 ft.

    C. 1 3/4 ft.

    D. 2 ft.

6. What is the total length of the ribbons?

    A. 25 feet

    B. 25 3/4 feet

    C. 26 3/4 feet

    D. 25 1/4 feet

MEASUREMENT AND DATA

The list of fractions shows the length of cherries picked from the cherry tree in inches.

1/2   3/4   1/4   3/4   7/8   3/4   1/2   3/8   1/4   3/4   1/2   3/8

7. Use the data to complete the line plot below. Answer questions 8-10 using the line plot.

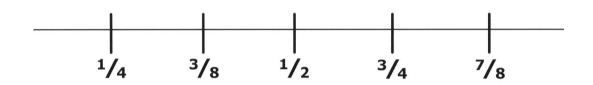

8. How many cherries are 1/2 inch in size or less?

    A. 5 cherries

    B. 6 cherries

    C. 8 cherries

    D. 7 cherries

9. What is the difference between the number of 1/2 inch cherries and the number of 7/8 inch cherries?

    A. 2 cherries

    B. 1 cherry

    C. 3 cherries

    D. 1/2 cherry

10. How many more inches are needed to make 7 inches total in length for the all the cherries combined?

    A. 1/4 inch

    B. 7/8 inch

    C. 3/8 inch

    D. 3/4 inch

MEASUREMENT AND DATA

11. Use the information in the chart to make a line plot. Label all parts of the line plot.

   The chart shows the number of miles run in physical education.

Student	1	2	3	4	5	6	7	8	9
Miles Run	$2\frac{1}{4}$	$1\frac{3}{4}$	$3\frac{1}{2}$	$2\frac{1}{4}$	$1\frac{3}{4}$	2	$2\frac{1}{4}$	$3\frac{3}{4}$	$3\frac{1}{2}$

12. Explain how you find the average number of miles run:

___

___

___

___

___

ASK & ANSWER QUESTIONS USING TEXT EVIDENCE

5.MD.C.3 Recognize volume as an attribute of solid figures and understand concepts of volume measurement.

5.MD.C.3.A A cube with side length 1 unit, called a "unit cube," is said to have "one cubic unit" of volume, and can be used to measure volume.

5.MD.C.3.B A solid figure which can be packed without gaps or overlaps using *n* unit cubes is said to have a volume of *n* cubic units.

---

1. Kelly is building a shape using 1-inch cubes. What is the volume of her shape?

   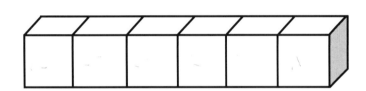

   A. 5 cubic inches
   B. 6 cubic inches
   C. 7 cubic inches
   D. 8 cubic inches

2. If Sherry uses 4 of these inch unit cubes to make a square, what is the volume of her shape?

   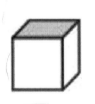

   A. 44 cubic inches
   B. 40 cubic inches
   C. 4 cubic inches
   D. 14 cubic inches

3. Tommy builds this shape with 1-inch unit cubes. What is the volume of his shape?

   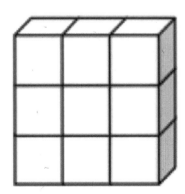

   A. 9 cubic inches
   B. 8 cubic inches
   C. 10 cubic inches
   D. 12 cubic inches

4. Eric builds this shape with 1-inch unit cubes. What is the volume of his shape?

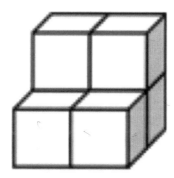

A. 5 cubic inches
B. 4 cubic inches
C. 8 cubic inches
D. 6 cubic inches

5. Ron builds a shape using 2 layers of the 1-inch unit cubes shown below. What is the volume of his shape?

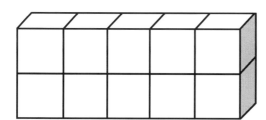

A. 10 cubic inches
B. 14 cubic inches
C. 12 cubic inches
D. 11 cubic inches

6. Corey uses 1-inch unit cubes to build this figure. What is the volume of his shape?

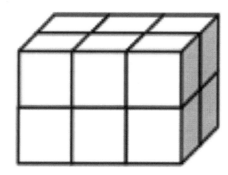

A. 14 cubic inches
B. 10 cubic inches
C. 12 cubic inches
D. 13 cubic inches

7. Denzel builds a rectangle that has 4 1-inches cubes in length and 5 1-inches cubes in width. What is the volume of the rectangle Denzel built?

A. 22 cubic inches
B. 20 cubic inches
C. 18 cubic inches
D. 15 cubic inches

MEASUREMENT AND DATA

8. What is the volume of this shape?

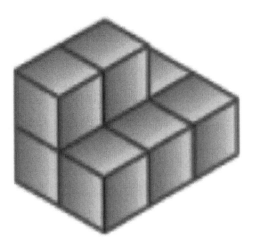

A. 10 cubic inches
B. 9 cubic inches
C. 7 cubic inches
D. 8 cubic inches

9. The first layer of Gerald's shape has 6 1-inch cubes, the middle layer has 5 1-inch cubes, and the top layer is half of the bottom layer. What is the volume of Gerald's shape?

   A. 12 cubic inches
   B. 11 cubic inches
   C. 14 cubic inches
   D. 15 cubic inches

10. Draw two different shapes on the pegboard that have a volume of 12 cubic units.

Shape A

Shape B

11. What is the volume of this shape in cubic inches?

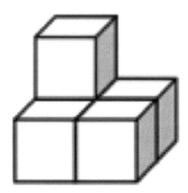

Answer:_____

Explain how you determined the volume of the shape.

_____

_____

12. Keenan builds this shape with 1-inch cubes. If he adds a layer of cubes to cover the bottom layer, what is the volume of the shape?

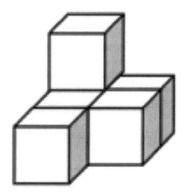

Answer:_____

Explain you determined the volume of the shape.

_____

_____

MEASURE VOLUME BY COUNTING CUBES

5.MD.C.4 Measure volumes by counting unit cubes, using cubic cm, cubic in, cubic ft, and improvised units.

1. What is the volume of the shape below in cubic centimeters?

   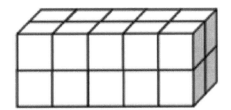

   A. 15 cubic cm.
   B. 20 cubic cm.
   C. 24 cubic cm.
   D. 16 cubic cm.

2. What is the volume of the shape below in cubic feet?

   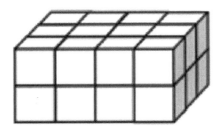

   A. 24 cubic ft.
   B. 18 cubic ft.
   C. 20 cubic ft.
   D. 22 cubic ft.

3. Katie is counting the horizontal layers in this shape. How many layers are in this shape?

   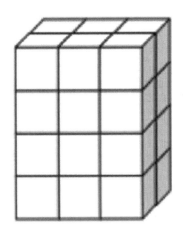

   A. 4 layers of 3 cubes
   B. 3 layers of 4 cubes
   C. 4 layers of 6 cubes
   D. 3 layers of 6 cubes

4. Sally folds this shape to make a rectangular box with each box representing 1 cubic inch. The 4 shaded cubes represent the bottom layer. How many 1-inch cubes will fit into the box?

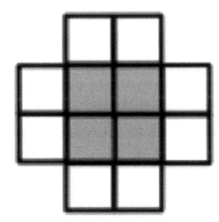

A. 6 one-inch cubes
B. 4 one-inch cubes
C. 12 one-inch cubes
D. 8 one-inch cubes

5. What is the volume of this box when it's completely full with 1-inch cubes?

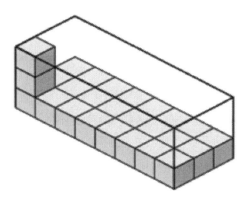

A. 63 cubic inches
B. 70 cubic inches
C. 68 cubic inches
D. 72 cubic inches

6. What is the volume of this box when it's completely full with 1-inch cubes?

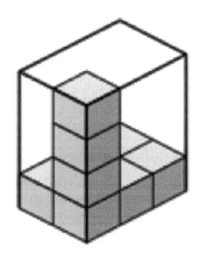

A. 24 cubic inches
B. 20 cubic inches
C. 22 cubic inches
D. 26 cubic inches

7. Arthur folds the figure to make a box and fills the box with 1-centimeter cubes. The shaded cubes represent the bottom of the box. How many cubes will fill the box?

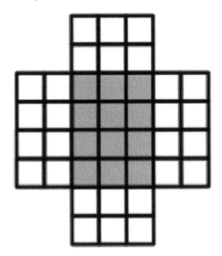

A. 22
B. 48
C. 24
D. 32

8. What is the volume of this shape in cubic units?

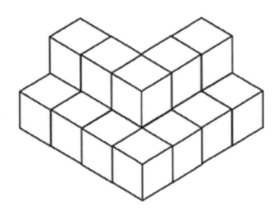

A. 19 cubic units
B. 17 cubic units
C. 16 cubic units
D. 18 cubic units

9. What is the volume of this shape in cubic units?

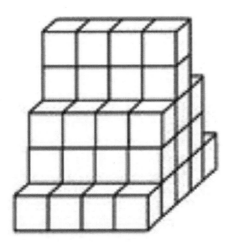

A. 48 cubic units
B. 50 cubic units
C. 44 cubic units
D. 52 cubic units

10. Draw a shape with 2 layers that has a volume of 36 cubic units.

Layer 1   **Layer 2**

11. Explain how to find the volume when this shape is folded to make an open box.

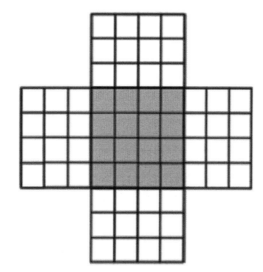

Volume: _____

_____

_____

_____

_____

MEASUREMENT AND DATA

12. Explain how to find the volume of this shape.

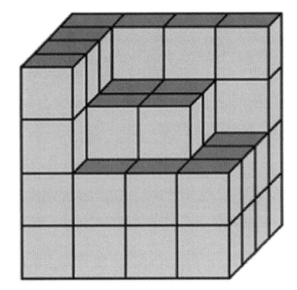

Volume: _____

_____

_____

_____

_____

SOLVE PROBLEMS INVOLVING VOLUME

5.MD.C.5 Relate volume to the operations of multiplication and addition and solve real world and mathematical problems involving volume.

5.MD.C.5.A Find the volume of a right rectangular prism with whole-number side lengths by packing it with unit cubes, and show that the volume is the same as would be found by multiplying the edge lengths, equivalently by multiplying the height by the area of the base. Represent threefold whole-number products as volumes, e.g., to represent the associative property of multiplication.

5.MD.C.5.B Apply the formulas $V = l \times w \times h$ and $V = b \times h$ for rectangular prisms to find volumes of right rectangular prisms with whole-number edge lengths in the context of solving real world and mathematical problems

5.MD.C.5.C Recognize volume as additive. Find volumes of solid figures composed of two non-overlapping right rectangular prisms by adding the volumes of the non-overlapping parts, applying this technique to solve real world problems.

1. What is the volume of this rectangular prism in cubic inches?

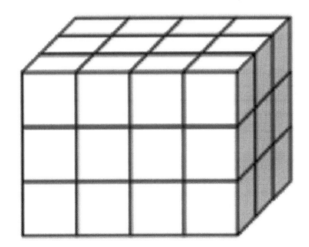

- **A.** 32 cubic inches
- **B.** 26 cubic inches
- **C.** 36 cubic inches
- **D.** 38 cubic inches

2. What is the volume of this rectangular prism? Choose the equation needed to solve.

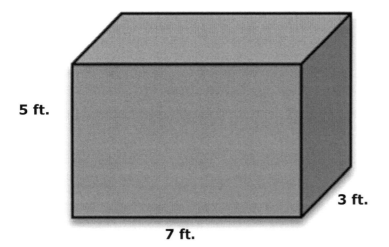

A. 5 x 7 x 3 =
B. 5 x 5 x 7 =
C. 5 x 3 x 5 =
D. 7 x 3 x 7 =

3. What is the volume of this rectangular prism?

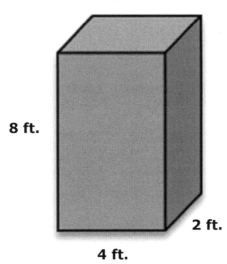

A. 68 cu. ft.
B. 64 cu. ft.
C. 80 cu. ft.
D. 60 cu. ft.

4. Each layer of this rectangular prism has an area of 14 sq. inches. What is the volume of the entire rectangle?

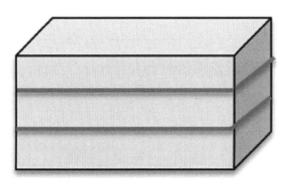

A. 32 cu. ft.
B. 40 cu. ft.
C. 38 cu. ft.
D. 42 cu. ft.

5. Find the volume of this rectangular prism.

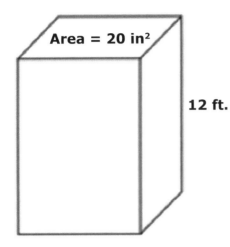

A. 240 cu. ft.
B. 140 cu. ft.
C. 120 cu. ft.
D. 220 cu. ft.

6. Kendra has a box for packing that is 2 feet wide, 3 feet tall and the length is double the width of the box. What is the volume of the box?
   A. 25 cu. ft.
   B. 30 cu. ft.
   C. 24 cu. ft.
   D. 22 cu. ft.

7. Jeremy is building a cube for storage. The cube has a length of 6 feet. What is the volume of the cube?
   A. 36. ft.
   B. 216 cu. ft.
   C. 116 cu. ft.
   D. 200 cu. ft.

8. Colby is solving a volume problem but he already knows the volume is 72 cubic inches. The length of the figure is 6 inches and the width of the figure 3 inches. What is the height of the shape?

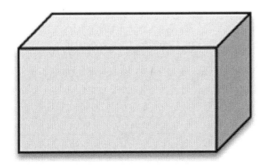

A. 6 inches
B. 5 inches
C. 3 inches
D. 4 inches

9. Find the volume of the shape.

A. 72 cubic inches
B. 52 cubic inches
C. 20 cubic inches
D. 70 cubic inches

10. The base area of the turtle tank is 48 sq. inches. The tank is filled with water to a depth of 15 inches. If the height of tank is 26 inches, what is the remaining volume of the tank that is not filled with water?

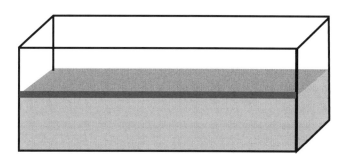

Answer: _____

11. Jordan wants to make 3 different garden boxes that each have a volume of 360 cubic feet. What could be the 3 different dimensions of the boxes?

Show your work:

   Part A. Box 1 dimensions: _____

   Part B. Box 2 dimensions: _____

   Part C. Box 3 dimensions: _____

12. Sarah has a rectangular prism with a volume of 160 cubic inches.

    Part A. Nicole's rectangular prism volume is $1/2$ of Sarah's volume. What could be the dimensions of Nicole's rectangular prism?

    _____

    _____

    Part B. Nicole needs to double the volume of her rectangular prism. Should she double the dimensions of the rectangular prism? Explain.

    _____

    _____

    _____

13. Amirdara creates a box in the shape of a rectangular prism with the following dimensions: 12 inches by 9 inches by 6 inches. The box will hold 3 inch by 3 inch by 3 inch blocks. What is the largest number of blocks that will fit in the box? Explain using words and numbers.

    _____

    _____

    _____

    _____

GEOMETRY

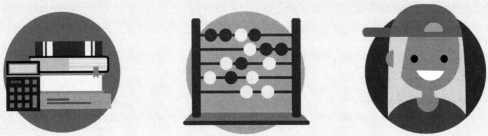

UNDERSTAND GRAPH POINTS ON THE COORDINATE PLANE

5.G.A.1 Use a pair of perpendicular number lines, called axes, to define a coordinate system, with the intersection of the lines (the origin) arranged to coincide with the 0 on each line and a given point in the plane located by using an ordered pair of numbers, called its coordinates. Understand that the first number indicates how far to travel from the origin in the direction of one axis, and the second number indicates how far to travel in the direction of the second axis, with the convention that the names of the two axes and the coordinates correspond (e.g., x-axis and x-coordinate, y-axis and y-coordinate).

1. Identify point A on the number line.

- **A.** 3/4
- **B.** 2/3
- **C.** 1 1/2
- **D.** 1 3/4

2. What is the distance of point B from the origin zero?

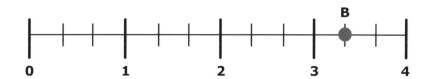

- **A.** 3 1/3
- **B.** 3 2/3
- **C.** 3
- **D.** 3 1/4

GEOMETRY

Use the graph below to answer questions 3-12.

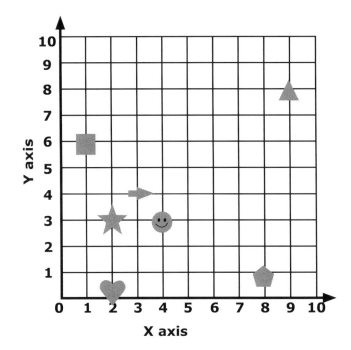

3. What is the first coordinate for the pentagon?
    A. 1
    B. 81
    C. 8
    D. 18

4. What is the coordinate on the Y-axis for the square?
    A. 16
    B. 6
    C. 61
    D. 1

5. Name the shape at the coordinate (3, 4).
    A. heart
    B. arrow
    C. smiley face
    D. star

6. Which shape is located at 4 on the X-axis?
    A. heart
    B. arrow
    C. smiley face
    D. star

7. Which coordinates identifies the star?
   - **A.** (2, 3)
   - **B.** (3, 2)
   - **C.** (3, 3)
   - **D.** (2, 2)

8. Which two shapes have the same X coordinate?
   - **A.** heart and square
   - **B.** arrow and star
   - **C.** smiley face and star
   - **D.** star and heart

9. Which two shapes have the same Y coordinate?
   - **A.** heart and square
   - **B.** arrow and star
   - **C.** smiley face and star
   - **D.** star and heart

10. Name the coordinates for:

    The triangle: _____

    The heart: _____

    The pentagon: _____

11. Carla says the smiley face can be labeled as (3, 4) and (4, 3). Is she correct? Explain your thinking.

    _____

    _____

    _____

12. Which 2 shapes are 2 units away from each other on the Y-axis and have y-coordinates of more than 3?

    Shapes: _____

    Name the coordinates for these shapes: _____

    Shapes: _____

    Name the coordinates for these shapes: _____

GEOMETRY

SOLVE PROBLEMS USING COORDINATE PLANE

5.G.A.2 Represent real world and mathematical problems by graphing points in the first quadrant of the coordinate plane, and interpret coordinate values of points in the context of the situation.

Use the coordinate grid below to solve #1-3.

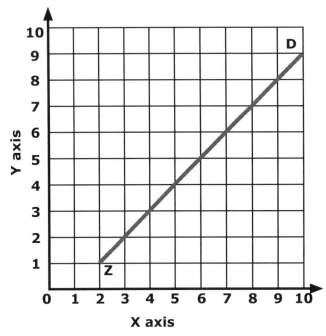

1. Which ordered pair below is on line DZ?
   - **A.** (2, 2)
   - **B.** (3, 2)
   - **C.** (4, 5)
   - **D.** (8, 6)

2. Which ordered pair below is NOT on line DZ?
   - **A.** (2, 1)
   - **B.** (6, 5)
   - **C.** (9, 8)
   - **D.** (6, 7)

3. What is the rule that generates the line DZ?
   - **A.** $x - 1 = y$
   - **B.** $x + 1 = y$
   - **C.** $y + 2 = x$
   - **D.** $y - 2 = x$

GEOMETRY

4. Jonah is working on doubling x and halving y using the ordered pair (4, 10). What is the resulting ordered pair?

   A. (2, 20)
   B. (8, 6)
   C. (8, 5)
   D. (6, 5)

Use the grid below to answer questions #5-8

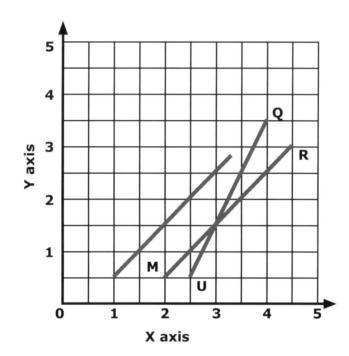

5. Which ordered pair intersects two lines?

   A. (3, 2)
   B. (3, 1 ½)
   C. (2, ½)
   D. (1 ½, 3)

6. Which ordered pair is on line QU?

   A. (3, 2)
   B. (4, 2 ½)
   C. (2, 1 ½)
   D. (4, 3 ½)

GEOMETRY

7. What is the rule that generates line RM?

   A. x − 1 1/2 = y
   B. x − 2 1/2 = y
   C. x − 1/2 = y
   D. x + 1 1/2 = y

8. What is the rule for a line that is parallel to line RM and crosses point (1, 1/2)?

   A. x − 1 1/2 = y
   B. x + 1/2 = y
   C. x − 1/2 = y
   D. x + 1 1/2 = y

9. What is the rule for a line that contains the points (1 1/2, 3) and (3, 4 1/2)?

   A. x − 1 1/2 = y
   B. x + 2 1/2 = y
   C. x + 1/2 = y
   D. x + 1 1/2 = y

10. Plot the points and ordered pairs on the coordinate grid below. Connect the points to make a line.

Point	X-coordinate	Y-coordinate
C	1 1/2	2
Z	2	3
E	2 1/2	4

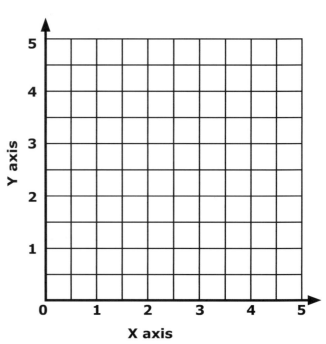

11. Create a table for the X and Y coordinates where the Y-coordinate is 2 times the X-coordinate. Plot your 3 ordered pairs on the coordinate grid.

X-coordinate	Y-coordinate	(X, Y)

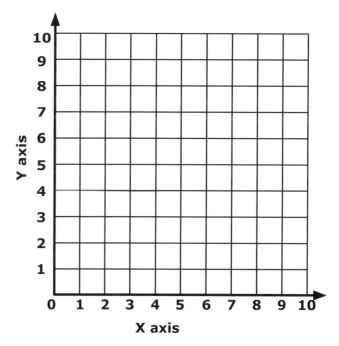

12. Generate a rule for a line that passes through $(1 \frac{1}{2}, 3)$ and plot 3 points using that rule on the coordinate grid below.

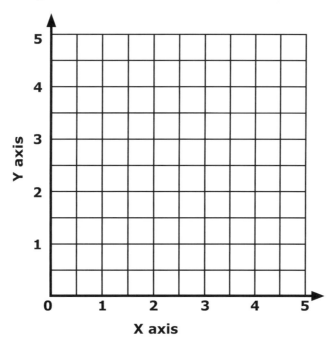

GEOMETRY

UNDERSTAND ATTRIBUTES OF TWO-DIMENSIONAL SHAPES

5.G.B.3 Understand that attributes belonging to a category of two-dimensional figures also belong to all subcategories of that category. For example, all rectangles have four right angles and squares are rectangles, so all squares have four right angles.

---

1. Which statement about quadrilateral is always true?
    A. Rectangles are always squares
    B. Squares are always rectangles
    C. Trapezoids have 4 right angles
    D. Rhombuses are always squares

    4 right angles and 2 pair parralel sides

2. If a right triangle has one angle that measures 90°, what must be true about the other 2 angles?
    A. Each of the other 2 angles must be less than 90°
    B. The sum of the other 2 angles must be more than 90°
    C. The other 2 angles are obtuse angles
    D. The other 2 angles are right angles

    3 angles in triangle = 180°

3. Which polygon fits the definition of 3 sides and 3 angles of different measures?
    A. equilateral triangle
    B. isosceles triangle
    C. scalene triangle
    D. right triangle

    legs equal length

4. Which statement below about quadrilaterals is false?
    A. A rhombus is also a parallelogram
    B. A square is also a rhombus
    C. A rectangle is also a quadrilateral
    D. A trapezoid is also a square

    trapezoid has 1 pair of parralel sides
    square has 2 pairs

5. Which statement below about a regular hexagon is false?
    A. All angles will have different measures
    B. All angles are congruent
    C. All sides are congruent
    D. It has 3 pairs of parallel sides

    in a regular hexagon, all sides and angles are congruent.

6. Choose the terms that describe this polygon.

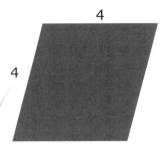

   A. parallelogram, quadrilateral, square
   B. rhombus, quadrilateral, parallelogram
   C. rectangle, rhombus, parallelogram
   D. quadrilateral, rectangle, rhombus

7. Which polygon can have 1 pair of parallel sides and 2 right angles?
   A. trapezoid
   B. rhombus
   C. equilateral triangle
   D. parallelogram

8. What defines an isosceles trapezoid?
   A. It has no parallel sides
   B. It has 3 congruent angles
   C. The two base angles are congruent
   D. It has 2 pairs of parallel sides

9. When can a parallelogram also be labeled as a rectangle?
   A. If the parallelogram has 4 acute angles
   B. If the parallelogram has 4 sides of equal length
   C. If the parallelogram has 2 right angles
   D. If the parallelogram has 4 right angles

10. Write in the Venn diagram the names of the polygons that meet the requirements.

    square   rectangle   rhombus   trapezoid   right triangle
    At least 1 pair of parallel sides   At least 1 right angle

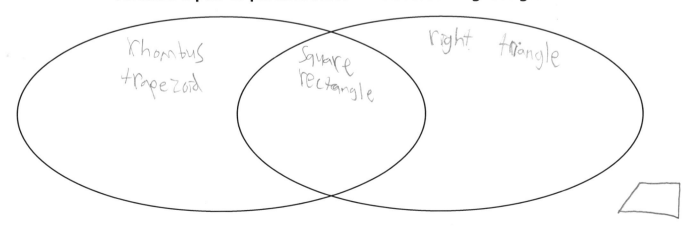

11. Draw the polygons below on the grid using a ruler.

   A. Draw a rhombus with no right angles

   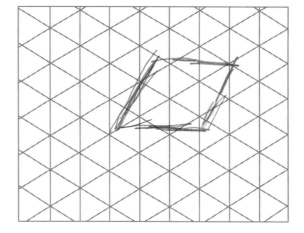

   B. Draw a rhombus with 4 right angles

   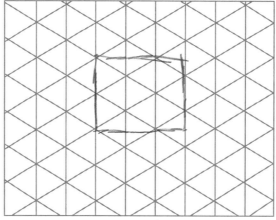

   a. What is another name for this polygon? __square__

   C. Draw a rectangle with adjacent sides that are not equal

   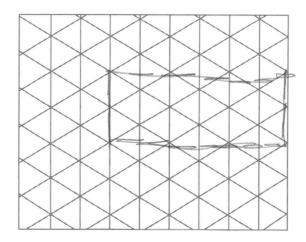

D. Draw a rectangle with 4 congruent sides

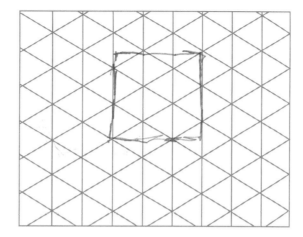

a. What is another name for this polygon? __Square__

12. Kim says a square is always a rhombus and a rectangle but a rhombus or a rectangle is not always a square. Is she correct? Explain your reasoning.

Yes.

CLASSIFY TWO-DIMENSIONAL SHAPES

5.G.B.4 Classify two-dimensional figures in a hierarchy based on properties.

1. Which polygon does not have any parallel sides?
    A. rhombus
    B. regular hexagon
    C. trapezoid
    D. regular pentagon

2. Which polygon has 3 sides that are all different lengths?
    A. isosceles triangle
    B. equilateral triangle
    C. scalene triangle
    D. regular triangle

3. Which polygon below has 4 congruent sides and no right angles?

   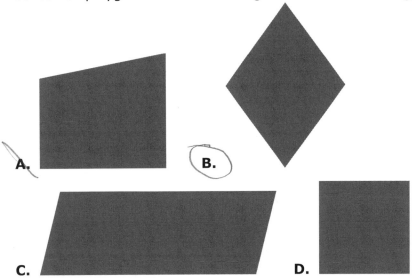

4. What characteristic do these polygons share?

   square, equilateral triangle, regular octagon

    A. All sides are congruent
    B. All angles are right angles
    C. All sides are parallel
    D. All angles are obtuse angles

5. What is similar about the shapes below?

    A. They have the same number of angles
    B. They have 1 pair of parallel sides
    C. They each have obtuse angles
    D. They have at least 1 right angle

6. A triangle has sides that measure 12 feet, 18.5 feet, and 12 feet. What type of triangle is this?
    A. isosceles triangle
    B. equilateral triangle
    C. scalene triangle
    D. regular triangle

7. Which polygon can have sides of any length but must have 1 set of parallel sides?
    A. rhombus
    B. trapezoid
    C. scalene triangle
    D. octagon

8. Which polygon has 2 sets of opposite angles that are of equal measure?
    A. pentagon
    B. trapezoid
    C. parallelogram
    D. equilateral triangle

9. The perimeter of a rhombus is 212 inches. What is the length of one side?
    A. 50 inches
    B. 55 inches
    C. 54 inches
    D. 53 inches

10. Draw an equilateral triangle using cm or in. Explain how you know it's equilateral.

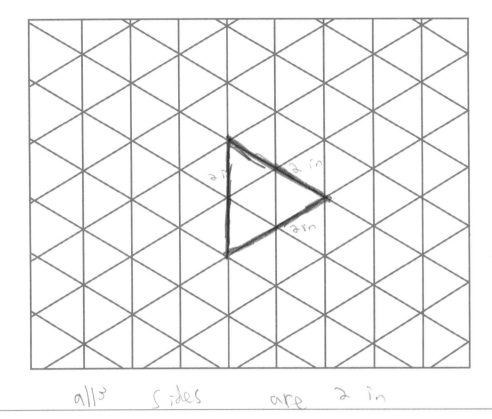

all 3 sides are 2 in

11. A parallelogram has an area of 24 inches. Draw one such parallelogram.

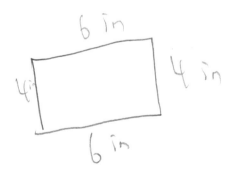

Length/Base : 6   Height : 4

12. Draw an isosceles trapezoid in inches or centimeters.

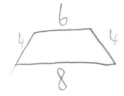

Explain how you can prove this trapezoid is an isosceles trapezoid.

The left side and right sides are equal.

ANSWER KEY

 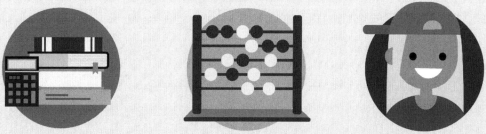 

OPERATIONS AND ALGEBRAIC THINKING

5.OA.A.1 Evaluate Numerical Expressions

1. B. Following the order of operations. (5 + 3) must be completed first since it is in parentheses.

2. C. After completing the first part in parentheses (21 + 2), then subtract 85 – 23 since there are brackets surrounding that section.

3. A. The first two steps are completed in the parentheses: (12- 3 x 3)

The equation is now 7 x 2 – 4 + 3 so 7 x 2 is the third step.

4. D. Follow the order of operations to solve: PEMDAS

(9 x 2 – 4) – 20 ÷ 5 =

(18 – 4) – 20 ÷ 5

14 – 20 ÷ 5

14 – 4 = 10

5. B. Follow the order of operations to solve: PEMDAS

31 + (14 – 2 x 3) x 2

31 + (14 – 6) x 2

31 + 8 x 2

31 + 16

6. A. (36 – 6) ÷ 5

Carson keeps 6 sticks of gum for himself so first subtract 36 – 6. He has 30 pieces left to share with 5 friends so divide by 5 : 30 ÷ 5

7. C. Follow the order of operations to solve: PEMDAS

3 x {[6 + 10 - (7 + 3) - 2] + 5}

3 x {[6 + 10 - 10- 2] + 5}

3 x {[16 - 10- 2] + 5}

3 x {[6- 2] + 5}

3 x { 4+ 5}

3 x 9 = 27

8. D. The next step needed to solve would be to solve the expression in parentheses first:

30 + 8 ÷ 2 – **(10 + 2)** =

30 + 8 ÷ 2 - **12**

9. B. 7 x (5 + 8)

First, find the number of miles Maggie bikes each day (5 + 8). Then multiply by the number of days in a week, 7, to find the total number of miles Maggie biked in a week.

10. 24 + {[3 + (8 x 2) – 6] x 2}

24 + {[3 + 16 – 6] x 2}

24 + {[19 – 6] x 2}

24 + {13x 2}

24 + 26 = 50

Follow the order of operations to solve starting with the parentheses, then brackets then braces.

11. Part A -

1. B.
2. C.
3. A.

Part B-

1. 33 pages
2. 21 dollars
3. 8 dollars

Marshall has $6 and spent $3 on a smoothie. Then he found $5 in his car. So first subtract 6-3, then add 5 since he found $5

Mary reads 5 pages of her book after breakfast and 6 pages after dinner for 3 days. First add the number of pages read each day 5 + 6 =11 then multiply by 3 since she read 11 pages for 3 days = 33

Bryant bought 3 bags of candy for $5 each and a toy for $6. First, multiply to find the cost of the 3 bags of candy, 3 x 5 = 15. Then add 6 to find how much money he spend 15 + 6 = $21

12. Part A - 20 – [(2 x 3) + (2 x 4) + 2]

Part B - No, he has $4 leftover and a notebook costs $5

Part C- Harry can purchase 1 pack of markers, 2 rulers or 1 binder.

First put the cost of the 2 binders and 2 packs of markers in parentheses: binders (2 x 3) markers (2 x 4) then add the ruler:

[(2 x 3) + (2 x 4) + 2]

Finally subtract to find the amount of money remaining:

20 – [(2 x 3) + (2 x 4) + 2] = 4

5.OA.A.2 Write & Interpret Numerical Expressions

1. B. 3 times as much as 2= 3 x 2, then add 16

(3 x 2) + 16

2. C. 4 times as much as the sum of three-hundred twenty-one and one hundred ninety.

3. D. 30 x 32 − 32

30 thirty-twos is the same as 30 groups of 32 so multiply 30 x 32 then subtract 32

30 x 32 - 32

4. A. 15 + (7 x 21)

7 packs of 21 cards means multiply 7 x 21 to find the total number of cards. Then add 15 for the last pack of cards.

5. D. First find the number of cupcakes by multiplying 4 x 12 since there are 4 trays with 12 cupcakes on each tray. Then divide by 16 because the cupcakes were shared by 16 people (4 x 12) ÷ 16

6. B. 45 − (8 x 5)

First find the number of stickers he gave away: 8 friends get 5 stickers each (8 x 5). Then subtract 45 − 40 or (8 x 5) to find the amount remaining.

7. C. First subtract to find the number of pages Cara has left to read, (180 − 40). Then, divide by 7 to find the number of pages she needs to read in the next 7 days. (180 − 40) ÷ 7

8. A. [(7 x 6) − 10] ÷ 4

First find the number of cookies Marco made 7 x 6. Then subtract 10 because he keeps 10 for himself [(7 x 6) − 10]. Finally, divide by 4 because he shared 4 cookies with each friend.

9. D. c = 30n + 80

To find the cost for the number of people attending the event, multiply the cost of each person by the number of people 30n. Then add 80 for the room fee.

10. 3 seventeens, tripled <

4 times the sum of 18 and 29

3 seventeens = 3 x 17 = 51. 51 tripled = 51 x 3 = 153. The sum of 18 and 29 = 18 + 29 = 47, times 4 = 47 x 4 = 188

11. Part A - 4 x 5.50

Part B- No, see explanation

The first step is to find the cost of the 4 sandwiches for 5.50 each

B. 4 x 5.50 + 1.95 = $23.95, Subtract 25.00 − 23.95 = $1.05 so no she does not have enough money .

12. Part A- [(8 x 12) x 3] − 150

Part B- $138

[(8 x 12) x 3] − 150 =

First find how much money he makes a week: 8 x 12, then multiply by 3 because he saves for 3 weeks. Then subtract 150 to find the amount of money remaining.

He will have $138 remaining.

5.OA.B.3 Use Numerical Patterns & Graph Ordered Pairs in Coordinate Plane

1. C. (5, 8) is a pair shown on the table so that pair would be on the coordinate grid.

2. A. The rule for this pattern is x + 2 = y because 1 + 2 = 3, 3 + 2 = 5. Choice A (8, 10) shows the same pattern 8 + 2 = 10

3. C. The pattern for x is x + 4

The pattern for y is y + 6

So add 4 to the x pattern and 6 to the y pattern to get (22, 35).

4. D. The 6th term in the first pattern is 17 and the 6th term in the second pattern is 13, 17-13 = 4

5. A. Sue's pattern: 27, 24, 21, 28, 15

John's pattern: 32, 28, 24, 20, 16

6. B. n x 15 = d because multiply the number of hours times 15 to find the amount of money it costs to rent a car.

2 x 15 = 20

4 x 15 = 60

7. C. Pattern B is two times as much as Pattern A because each number in Pattern B is twice as much as the corresponding number in Pattern A: 3 x 2 = 6, 6 x 2 = 12 and so on.

8. A. The ordered pair is (5, 7) because looking at the pattern: x + 2 = y so 5 + 2 = 7.

9. D. The temperature starts at 160 and drops 12 degrees 3 times.

160 starting time

148 8 minutes (-12)

136 16 minutes (-12)

124 24 minutes (-12)

10. Part A- p x 4 = c

Part B- 15 pizzas cost $60

The relationship between the two numbers is p x 4 = c. 3 x 4 = 12, 6 x 4 = 24

Using the equation p x 4 = c: 15 pizzas x 4 = $60

11. Benjamin: 3, 6, 9, 12, 15

Luke: 9, 18, 27, 36, 45

Luke saves 3 times as much as Benjamin. Benjamin

saves 3 dollars per day and Luke says 9, which is 3 times more than Benjamin: 3 (Benjamin's amount) x 3 =9 (Luke's amount).

12. y = 3x

1 x 3 = 3 (1, 3)

2 x 3 = 6 (2, 6)

3 x 3 = 9 (3 , 9)

4 x 3 = 12 (4, 12)

y = 2x + 1

1 x 2 = 2 + 1 = 3 (1, 3)

2 x 2 = 4 + 1 = 5 (2, 5)

3 x 2 = 6 + 1 = 7 (3, 7)

4 x 2 = 8 + 1 = 9 (4, 9)

Follow the equations to see how the answers for the x and y columns were created.

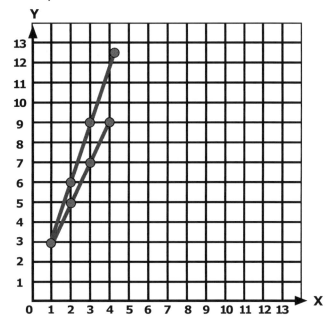

NUMBERS AND OPERATIONS IN BASE TEN

5.NBT.A.1 Understand Place Value

1. C. 10 times as much is the same as 10 x 100 = 1000

2. B. 10 times 4,000 is 40,000

10 x 4,000 = 40,000

3. D. One hundred times as much means 100 x 100 x 1,360 = 136,000

4. A. one-tenth of is the same as dividing by 10

5. B. $1/100$ is the same as dividing by 100. 1.2 divided by 100 is moving 2 places values to left = 0.012

6. C. 430 divide by 10 equals 43

7. D. 100 x 0.072 moves the decimal two places values to the right = 7.2 cm

8. A. 1000 x 0.529 = 529, move the decimal three place values to the right because multiplying means the number is increasing.

9. B. 12,000,000 divided by 10 is 1,200,000 or 1.2 million. one-tenth of is the same as dividing by 10.

10. The 5 in 152,378 is in the ten thousands place. The 5 in 24,589 is in the hundreds place. 5 ten thousand is 100 times as much as 500 because 500 x 100 = 50,000

11. Part A/B/C-- In 6,245.39, the 3 is in the tenths place and is worth $3/10$ and in 364.5 the 3 is in the hundreds place and is worth 300. Therefore the 3 in the 6,245.39 has the smaller place value.

Part D- 300 is 1000 times as much as 0.3 because 0.3 x 1000 moves the decimal 3 place values to the left, which places the 3 in the hundreds place.

12. 30 hundredths is the same as multiplying 30 x 0.01 = 0.3

3 thousandths is equal to 0.003 in decimal form.

0.3 is not equal to 0.003 so Carl is incorrect. 3 hundreds or 3 groups of 100 is the same as 3 x 100 = 3,000 which is the same as 3 thousands. Multiplying by a decimal is not the same as multiplying by a whole number. Multiplying by 0.1 is the same as dividing by 10 on the place value chart.

Another way to write 30 hundredths is 0.3 because 30 groups of 0.01 is the same as 30 x 0.01 = 0.3

5.NBT.A.2 Powers of 10

1. C. 10 to the 4th power means multiply 10 4 times: 10 x 10 x 10 x 10 = 10,000.

2. D. 2.34 x 10³

10 to the third power means multiply 10 3 times, 10 x 10 x 10 = 1,000

1,000 x 2.34 = 2,340 because you move the decimal point 3 place values (10 x 10 x 10) to the right, the number is increasing when multiplying by 10s

3. A. 542.8 ÷ 10²

10 to the second power means 10 x 10 = 100

542.8 ÷ 100 moves the decimal 2 place values (10 x 10) to the left because dividing by 10 decreases the decimal. 542.8 ÷ 100 = 5.428

4. C. 100 x 1,000 = 100,000

100,000 written in base 10 is 10 x 10 x 10 x 10 x 10 or 10 5 times, which is 10^5

5. B. 145,000 ÷ 10^6

145,000 ÷ 1,000,000 = 0.145 move the decimal 6 place values to the left because dividing by base 10 decreases the value of the number.

6. B. The pattern is decreasing by 10^2 or 100. Each number is divided by 100

8,700,000 ÷ 100 = 87,000

87,000 ÷ 100 = 870

870 ÷ 100 = 8.7

7. D. 3.687 → 3,687

3.687 x 1,000 moves the decimal 3 places values to the right because 10 x 10 x 10 = 1,000 and numbers increase when multiplying by base 10

8. A. (4 x 10^3) + (0.5 x 10^2) + (35 x $1/100$) + (6 x $1/1000$) =

4 x 10^3 = 4 x 1000 = 4000

0.5 x 10^2 = 0.5 x 100 = 50

35 x $1/100$ = 35 x 0.01 = 0.35

6 x $1/1000$ = 6 x 0.001 = 0.006

Add the products: 4,000 + 50 + 0.35 + 0.006 = 4,050.356

9. 2nd and 3rd Choices. 923.9 and 9.239

923.9 ÷ 100 = 9.239 because dividing by 100 is moving the decimal 2 place values (10 x 10) to the left because the number is decreasing when dividing.

65.7 and 0.657

65.7 ÷ 100 = 0.657 because dividing by 100 is moving the decimal 2 place values (10 x 10) to the left because the number is decreasing when dividing.

10. Part A- No. 10^5 is 10 multiplied out 5 times: 10 x 10 x 10 x 10 x 10 = 100,000

100,000 is not the same as 500,000. Sam multiplied 100,000 x 5 to get 500,000.

Part B- 100,000

10^5 is 10 multiplied out 5 times: 10 x 10 x 10 x 10 x 10 = 100,000

11. Part A- 2.45 x 10^3 = 245,00 ÷ 10^2

Part B- 2,450 = 2,450 See explanation.

2.45 x 10^3 = 2.45 x 1,000 = 2,450 because multiplying by 1000 moves the decimal 3 place values (10 x 10 x 10) to the right. Multiplying by base 10 increases the number.

245,00 ÷ 10^2 = 245,000 ÷ 100 = 2,450 because dividing by 100 (10 x 10) moves the decimal 2 place values to the left.

Dividing by base 10 decreases the number.

2,450 = 2,450 so Mr. Holmes is correct.

12. Part A- 456 x 10^3 = 456,000

Part B- 456 ÷ 10^3 = 0.456

Part C- The numbers are different because one is multiplying by 1000 and the other is dividing by 1000. Multiplying by numbers in base 10 increases the number according to the number of place values multiplied. Dividing by numbers in base 10 decreases the number according to the number of place values divided.

456 x 10^3 = 456,000

456 x 10 x 10 x 10 = 456 x 1,000 = 456,000

456 ÷ 10^3 = 456 ÷ (10 x 10 x 10)

456 ÷ 1,000 = 0.456

5.NBT.A.3 Read, Write and Compare Decimals

1. B. 14.507 is written as fourteen and five hundred seven thousandths. "And" is written to show the decimal point and the decimal 0.507 is written as five hundred seven thousandths.

2. C. three and twenty-six thousandths is 3.026 in standard form. 0.026 is in the thousandths place.

3. D. 25.54 has a 4 in the hundredths place according to decimal place value 0.tenths 0.0hundredths, 0.00thousandths.

4. A. Point A represents 1.4 because the point is past the whole number 1 and the number line is divided into ten equal pieces or tenths so the decimal is 1.4 or one and 4 tenths.

5. B. 45.67 > 45.63 compare each place value: 4 tens, 5 ones, 6 tenths, 7 hundredths > 3 hundredths.

6. D. 4 x 100 = 400

5 x 1 = 5

$9 \times {}^1/_{10} = 0.9$

$4 \times {}^1/_{1000} = 0.004$

Add the products: 400 + 5 + 0.9 + 0.004 = 405.904

7. C. 6 x 10 = 60

4 x 1 = 4

$5 \times {}^1/_{10} = 0.5$

$8 \times {}^1/_{100} = 0.08$

Add the products: 60 + 4 + 0.5 + 0.08 = 64.58

8. A. 2.8 ÷ 10^3

10^3 = 10 x 10 x 10 = 1,000

2.8 ÷ 1,000 = 0.0028, which is the smallest decimal in the choices above.

9. B. 3.478, 3,48, 3.5
In 3.478, 7 hundredths is less than 8 hundredths.
In 3.48, 4 tenths is less than 5 tenths.

10. 4 and 5 tenths > 0.45

9.322 > 09.232

$0.6 > 6 \times {}^1/_{100}$

$0.038 < {}^{38}/_{100}$

4 and 5 tenths = 4.5 > 0.45 4 ones is greater than 0 ones.

9.322 > 09.232 3 tenths is greater than 2 tenths.

$0.6 > 6 \times {}^1/_{100} = 0.06$

0.6 > 0.06 6 tenths is greater than 0 tenths.

$0.038 < {}^{38}/_{100} = 0.38$

0.038 < 0.38 3 tenths is greater than 0 tenths.

11. Part A: 94.532 =

$(9 \times 10) + (4 \times 1) + (5 \times {}^1/_{10}) + (3 \times {}^1/_{100}) + (2 \times {}^1/_{1000})$

Part B: ninety-four and five hundred thirty-two thousandths.

12. Part A: 56.7 ÷ 100 = 0.567

Part B: $56.7 \times {}^1/_{100} = 0.567$

Part C- Multiplying by ${}^1/_{100}$ or dividing by 100 is the same operation because 5.67 = ${}^1/_{100}$ = ${}^{56.7}/_{100}$

56.7 over 100 is the same as dividing by 100 so the answers to part A and B are the same.

5.NBT.A.4 Rounding Decimals

1. B. 13.7 to the nearest ones places rounds to 14 because 13.7 is closer to 14 than 13

2. A. 6.43 is closer to 6.4 than 6.5 so it rounds to 6.4, the nearest tenths place.

3. D. 873.5 rounded to the nearest whole number is 874 because the 5 tenths places the number closer to 874 than 873

4. C. 14.472 rounded to the nearest hundredths place is 14.47 because the 2 in the thousands place does not change the number. Or think of hundredths place as 0.072 and rounded to 0.070

5. A. 23.57 rounds to 23.6 because 0.57 rounds to 0.6

6. B. 0.997 rounded to the nearest hundredths place is 1.0 because 7 in the thousandths rounds the 9 hundredths to 1 tenths, which rounds the 9 tenths t 1 whole.

7. D. 490.732 rounds to 490.73 because 0.732 rounds to 0.73 since it is closer to 0.73 than 0.74

8. C. 134.8348 rounds to 134.835 because 0.8348 is closer to 0.8350 than 0.8340

9. A. 72.54 rounds to 72.5 because 0.54 is closer to 0.50 than 0.60

and 72.54 rounds to 73.0 because 72.5 is closer to 73 than 72

10. Part A: 3.561 rounded to the nearest hundredths is 3.56

Part B: 3.561 rounded to the tenths place is 3.6

Part C: 3.561 rounded to the ones is 4

3.561 rounded to the nearest hundredths is 3.56 because 0.561 is closet to 0.56 than 0.57

3.561 rounded to the tenths place is 3.6 because 3.56 is closer to 3.6 than 3.5

3.561 rounded to the ones is 4 because 3.561 is closer to 4 than 3

11. Part A: 56.34

Part B: 56.25

56.34 (0.34 rounds to 0.3)is the largest possible number that rounds to 56.3 and 56.25 (0.25 rounds to 0.3) is the smallest possible number that rounds to 56.3

12. 0.946

Both Josh and Sandra are correct.

Josh rounds this amount to 0.95 liters and Sandra rounds this amount to 0.9

Josh rounded 0.946 to the nearest hundredths place, 0.95 and Sandra rounded 0.946 to the nearest tenths place, 0.9 so they each rounded to a different place value but their rounding is correct.

5.NBT.B.5 Multiply Multi-digit Whole Numbers

1. B. 63 x 3 = 189 and 100 x 10 = 1000 so 189 x 1000 = 189,000

2. C. 42 tens is the 42 x 10 = 420

4 hundreds is 4 x 100 = 400

420 x 400 = 168,000

3. A. 451 x 28 = 12,628

4. B. 90 x 42 = 3,780

5. C. 129 x 12 (12 months in one year) = 1,548

6. D. 60 x 30 = 1800

4 x 8 = 32, 1800 + 32 = 1832 is not equal to 64 x 38 = 2,432

7. A. 12,425 x 23 = 285,775 tickets.

8. B. 350 x 789 = 276,150

9. C. First add 145 + 58 since Janet earns $58 more than Marsha. Multiply (145 + 58) x 35 = $7,105

10. $3,060 James save 45 more than Carols so add 125 + 45 = 170, the amount James saves each month. If James saves 170 a month for 1.5 years, change 1.5 years into months by adding 12 (months in a year) + 6 (months in half a year) = 18. 170 x 18 = 3,060

11. $10,080;

$4,500

3 dogs a day for $20 each is $60 a day.

$60 a day for 168 = 168 x 60 = $10,080

5 dogs at $20 each is 5 x 20 = $100

$100 a day times 45 = $4,500

12. $1,358 total for the adult and student tickets;

Special exhibit and regular tickets = $3,002

25 adults at $14 a ticket = 25 x 14 = 350

112 student tickets at $9 a ticket = 112 x 9 = 1,008

350 + 1008 = 1358 total for the adult and student tickets.

112 + 25 = 137 adults and students.

137 people x $12 a ticket for the special exhibition = $1,644

1,644 + 1358 (price for regular tickets) = $3,002

5.NBT.B.6 Divide Whole Numbers

1. C. 400 + 50 + 7 = 457 which is then divided by 3 on the area model.

2. B. The reverse operation can be used to solve division. 25 x n = 3,465

3. D. 35,000 ÷ 700 = 50 because 50 x 700 = 35,000

4. A. 45,000 ÷ 5,000 = 9. 9 x 5,000 = 45,000 The total number of seats is 45,000, dividing by 5,000 to find the number od sections.

5. C. To find the missing length of the gym, divide the total 864 by the width 27. Area equals length x width so use the reverse operation to solve.

6. B. forty-eight hundred = 4800

24 x 200 = 4800, 4800 ÷ 24 = 200

7. D. 568 ÷ 32 = 17 remainder 24. In order to fit all the buttons into containers, she needs one more container 17 + 1 = 18, so she needs 18 containers to fit all the buttons.

8. A. 85 cupcakes divide by 13 classmates + herself = 14 people.

85 ÷ 14 = 6 remainder 1, so the 1 leftover cupcake will go to the teacher

9. C. (2,568 ÷12) x 14 =

The 2,568 cookies are divided into a dozen cookies per box (12). Each box is sold for $14 so multiply the quotient of (2,568 ÷12) by 14 to find the amount of money made on selling all the boxes.

10. Part A: 581

Part B: 581 ÷ 36 = 16 R 5

Part C: 36 x 16 = 576 + 5 = 581

A number divided by 36 has a quotient of 16 with a remainder of 5 is n ÷ 36 = 16 R 5

To find the dividend, use the inverse operation, multiplication, to solve. 36 x 16 = 576 + 5 (remainder)= 581

11. Part A: Thomas multiplied 16 x 200 = 3200. Then he subtracted 3280 - 3200 = 80 as his remainder. This is incorrect because 80 can further be divided into groups of 16. 80 ÷ 16 = 5, 5 x 16 = 80

Part B: 3280 ÷ 16 = 205

12. 6 round trip visits 25 minutes to the store plus 3 minutes to walk into the store = 25 + 3 = 28 minutes spent traveling to the store. A round trip visit means add the same amount of time to return home: 28 + 28 = 56 minutes spent traveling to the store and back. She spends 5 hours and 36 minutes each month traveling to the store, change

5 hours into minutes: 5 x 60 = 300 minutes but the remaining 36 minutes = 300 + 36 = 336 minutes each month. Divide 336 (total time spent traveling to the store each month) ÷ 56 minutes (the round trip time) = 6 round trips per month.

5.NBT.B.7 Add, Subtract, Multiply & Divide Decimals

1. B. 10^4 = 10 x 10 x 10 x 10 = 10,000

45.6 x 10^4 = 456,000

2. A. 10^3 = 10 x 10 x 10 = 1000

87.23 ÷ 10^3

87.23 ÷ 1000 = 0.08723

3. D. 0.3 x 0.5 = 0.15

0.3 is shaded vertically and 0.5 is shaded horizontally. 3 x 5 = 15 so 0.3 x 0.5 = 0.15. There are 15 out of 100 cubes shaded by the overlapping colors.

4. C. 15.95 + 8.75 = 24.70 spent on the sweater and scarf. Subtract to find the difference received in change: 30.00 - 24.70 = $5.30

5. C. 4 bags of flour for $6.69 each = 4 x 6.69 = 26.76

3 bags of chocolate chips for $3.55 = 3 x 3.55 = 10.65

26.76 + 10.65 = $37.41

6. D. Two-tenths of a number is the same as multiplying by 0.2 so multiply the population 40,000 x 0.2 = 8,000 people.

7. A. 0.8 ÷ 0.2 = 4

The remaining cake is 0.8. Divide the cake 0.8, into the 0.2 size pieces: 0.8 ÷ 0.2 = 4 so she can share with 4 friends.

8. C. A decimal times a decimal equals a product that will be less than the two factors.

0.2 x 0.4 = 0.08, 0.5 x 0.56 = 0.28, 0.6 x 0.09 = 0.054

9. A number in the tenths place times a number in the tenths place (example 0.2 x 0.3 = 0.06) equals a number in the hundredths place. One-tenth of a tenth or 0.1 x 0.1 = one one-hundredth (0.01) because $1/10$ x $1/10$ = $1/100$. The model below shows why this is true.

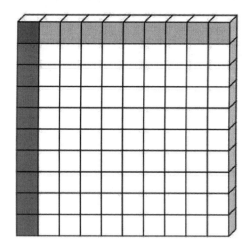

10. Part A: 7.56 feet

Part B: 20.412 sq. ft.

To find the length, multiply 5.4 x 1.4 = 7.56

To find the area of the first garden, multiply the length x width = 7.56 x 5.4 = 40.824 sq. ft.

Then divide the area by 2 (half) to find the area of the second garden = 40.824 ÷ 2 = 20.412 sq. ft.

11. Part A: 2.32 hours. 5.8 miles divide by the pace of 2.5 miles per hour = 5.8 ÷ 2.5 = 2.32 hours on Saturday.

Part B: 4.32 hours.

If she hiked the same amount 5.8 miles at a faster pace of 2.9 miles per hour, divide 5.8 ÷ 2.9 = 2 hours. 2 hours on Sunday + 2.32 hours on Saturday = 2 + 2.32 = 4.32 hours.

5.NF.A.1 NUMBERS AND OPERATIONS – FRACTIONS
Add and Subtract Fractions

1. B. $2/8 + 1/4 = 4/8$

Use a common denominator of 8

$1/4$ x $2/2$ = $2/8$ + $2/8$ = $4/8$

2. C. $1/3 + 1/6$

Use a common denominator of 6

$1/3$ x $2/2$ = $2/6$

$2/6 + 1/6 = 3/6$

3. A. The least common denominator for 5 and 6 is 30

5, 10, 15, 20, 25, 30

6, 12, 18, 24, 30

4. D. $3/4 + 2/6$

The least common denominator for 4 and 6 is 12

$3/4$ x $3/3$ = $9/12$

$2/6 \times 2/2 = 4/12$

5. A. The denominators 5, 8, and 20 all have a common multiple of 40, which is the least common multiple.

5, 10, 15, 20, 25 30, 35, 40

8, 16, 24, 32, 40

20, 40, 60

6. C. Subtract 2 and $2/3$ − 1 and $1/4$

Use the common denominator of 12

$2/3 \times 4/4 = 8/12$

$1/4 \times 3/3 = 3/12$

Subtract the whole numbers 2-1 = 1

Subtract the fractions $8/12 - 3/12 = 5/12$

1 and $5/12$

7. B. Subtract 1 $4/5$ - 1 $3/7$

Use a common denominator of 35

$4/5 \times 7/7 = 28/35$

$3/7 \times 5/5 = 15/35$

Subtract the whole numbers 1 − 1 = 0

Subtract the fractions $28/35 - 15/35 = 13/25$

8. D. Add $3/8 + 1/3 + 4/6$

Use a common denominator of 24

$3/8 \times 3/3 = 9/24$

$1/3 \times 8/8 = 8/24$

$4/6 \times 4/4 = 16/24$

$9/24 + 8/24 + 16/24 = 33/24 = 1$ and $9/24$

9. A. Add the amount of pasta already cooked: $1/2 + 2/5$

Use a common denominator of 10

$1/2 \times 5/5 = 5/10$

$2/5 \times 2/2 = 4/10$

$5/10 + 4/10 = 9/10$

1 or $10/10 - 9/10 = 1/10$ remaining.

10. Katie planted 1 and $3/20$ of the flower bed; See explanation. Subtract 1 $9/10 - 3/4$ to find the amount that Katie planted. Use a common denominator of 20

$9/10 \times 2/2 = 18/20$

$3/4 \times 5/5 = 15/20$

Subtract the whole numbers: 1-0 = 1

Subtract the fractions $18/20 - 15/20 = 3/20$

So the part Katie planted is 1 $3/20$

11. Part A: Add the amount of sugar she used:

1 $4/5$ + 2 $1/4$ + $2/10$

Use a common denominator of 20

$4/5 \times 4/4 = 16/20$

$1/4 \times 5/5 = 5/20$

$2/10 \times 2/2 = 4/20$

Add the whole numbers: 1 + 2 = 3

Add the fractions: $16/20 + 5/20 + 4/20 = 25/20 = 1$ $5/20$

Add the whole numbers and fractions: 1 + 3 = 4 $5/20$

Part B: $15/20$ or $3/4$ **cup of sugar remains.**

Subtract 5 − 4 $5/20$

Change 5 into 4 $20/20$

Subtract the whole numbers 4-4 = 0

Subtract the fractions $20/20 - 5/20 = 15/20$

Final answer: $15/20$ remains or simplified $15/20 \div 5/5 = 3/4$ cup of sugar.

12. Part A: Add the fractional amount of dollars spent.

Part B: Frank has 1 $17/24$ of his dollars remaining. Add 1 $1/6 + 3/8 + 1$ $3/4$

Use 24 as the LCD, least common denominator:

$1/6 \times 4/4 = 4/24$

$3/8 \times 3/3 = 9/24$

$3/4 \times 6/6 = 18/24$

Add the whole numbers 1 + 1 = 2

Add the fractions: $4/24 + 9/24 + 18/24 = 31/24 = 1$ $7/24$ plus 2 = 3 and $7/24$

Then subtract 5 − 3 $7/24$

Change 5 into 4 and $24/24$

Subtract 4 - 3 = 1

$24/24 - 7/24 = 17/24$ so the remaining fraction of dollars is 1 $17/24$

5.NF.A.2 Solve Word Problems Involving Subtraction & Addition of Fractions

1. C. 2 $1/4$ + 1 $1/2$

Use a common denominator of 4:

$1/2 \times 2/2 = 2/4$

Add the whole numbers:

2 + 1 = 3

Add the fractions $1/4 + 2/4 = 3/4$

ANSWER EXPLANATIONS

The sum is 3 and $3/4$

2. A. $3/8$ is close to $4/8$ which is $1/2$ and $1/5$ is close to zero to about $1/2 + 0 = 1/2$

3. D. Round $5/6$ to 1 whole since it is 5 out of 6 is close to 6 out of 6 or 1 whole. Round $2/5$ to $1/2$ because half of 5 is 2.5

4. A. To add $2/3 + 3/5$, change the fractions to have a common denominator of 15

$2/3 \times 5/5 = 10/15$
$3/5 \times 3/3 = 9/15$
$10/15 + 9/15 = 19/15$
$19/15 = 1$ and $4/15$

5. B. $1\ 1/6$ rounds to 1 and $4/5$ rounds to 1 so $1 + 1 = 2$ hours.

6. C. Subtract $3\ 7/8 - 2\ 2/6$

Use the common denominator 24
$7/8 \times 3/3 = 21/24$
$2/6 \times 4/4 = 8/24$
Subtract the whole numbers $3-2 = 1$
Subtract the fractions $21/24 - 8/24 = 13/24$
$1\ 13/24$

7. D. Add $1/3$ and $3/7$ to find how much Leo spent

Use the common denominator of 21
$1/3 \times 7/7 = 7/21$
$3/7 \times 3/3 = 9/21$
$7/21 + 9/21 = 16/21$

Subtract $21/21$ (1 whole) $- 16/21$ to find the amount remaining. $21/21 - 16/21 = 5/21$

8. A. First, add $1/4 + 1/8 + 2/12$ using the common denominator of 24
$1/4 \times 6/6 = 6/24$
$1/8 \times 3/3 = 3/24$
$2/12 \times 2/2 = 4/24$
$6/24 + 3/24 + 4/24 = 13/24$
Subtract the whole $24/24 - 13/24 = 11/24$

9. C. $5\ 1/7$ rounds to 5 because $1/7$ rounds to 0
$3\ 7/8$ rounds to 4 because $7/8$ rounds to 1 whole.
$4\ 3/6$ stays at $4\ 1/2$
Add $5 + 4 + 4\ 1/2 = 13\ 1/2$ feet.

10. 7 cups of flour. $2/6$ can be reduced to $1/3$ because $2/6 \div 2/2 = 1/3$
$2\ 1/3 + 2\ 1/3 + 2\ 1/3 =$
add the whole numbers $2 + 2 + 2 = 6$

add the fractions $1/3 + 1/3 + 1/3 = 3/3 = 1$
$6 + 1 = 7$ so she needs 7 cups of flour.

11. Part A: Joey Part B: 1 and $14/48$ hours
1 and $7/24$ hours. $10/12$ is larger than $4/6$ and $5/8$
Use the common denominator of 48 to compare:
$10/12 \times 4/4 = 40/48$
$4/6 \times 8/8 = 32/48$
$5/8 \times 6/6 = 30/48$
Add Mason and Kelly's time $4/6 + 5/8 =$
$4/6 \times 8/8 = 32/48$
$5/8 \times 6/6 = 30/48$
$32 + 30 = 62/48 = 1\ 14/48$
Part C: $1\ 7/24$

12. Part A: 1 and $2/3$ remains.
Part B: $23/30$ of the pizza. Add $1\ 1/6 + 1/10 + 2/5$
Use the common denominator of 30:
$1/6 \times 5/5 = 5/30$
$1/10 \times 3/3 = 3/30$
$2/5 \times 6/6 = 12/30$
Add $5 + 3 + 12 = 20/30$
$20/30$ can be simplified to $2/3$
$20/30 \div 10/10 = 2/3 + 1 = 1$ and $2/3$
$1\ 1/6 - 2/5$
Use the common denominator of 30
$1/6 \times 5/5 = 5/30$
$2/5 \times 6/6 = 12/30$
$1\ 5/30 - 12/30$
Borrow from the 1 whole to subtract $5 - 12$
$1 = 30/30 + 5/30 = 35/30$
$35/30 - 12/30 = 23/30$

5.NF.B.3 Divide Whole Numbers and Fractions

1. C. 1 divided into 4 pieces is the same as 1 shape or rectangle divided into 4 parts or $1/4$

Choice C has 1 out of 4 parts shaded and has 1 rectangle divided into 4 parts.

2. B. $1 \div 6$ is having one rectangle divided into 6 equal parts or $1/6$ as a fraction.

3. D. $2/3$ can be written as $2 \div 3$ as a division equation because 2 rectangles divided into thirds would show

$^2/_3$

4. A. Each person will receive 2 out of the 5 pieces because each pizza is divided into 5 pieces and since there are 2 pies, each person will receive $^2/_5$ of the pies.

5. C. 3 friends share 4 sandwiches so divide the 4 sandwiches between 3 people:

4 ÷ 3 = 1 and $^1/_3$

Each of the 4 sandwiches are split into 3 equal parts, so each person will receive $^4/_3$ or 1 and $^1/_3$

6. D. 5 bags of food divided between 6 dogs means divide each bag into 6 equal parts since there are 6 dogs. Each dog will get $^5/_6$ of the bag of food because 5 ÷ 6 = $^5/_6$

7. B. The boys will divide up the yard work so divide the yard 14, by the 3 boys.

14 ÷ 3 = 4 remainder 2, but the remaining 2 feet can be split between the 3 boys so each boy will do $^2/_3$ of the remaining 2 feet. Each boys will have 4 $^2/_3$ feet to work on.

8. A. She has 4 feet of ribbon that she needs to divide into 8 pieces so 4 ÷ 8 = $^4/_8$ or $^1/_2$ foot. Each piece will be $^1/_2$ foot long.

9. C. Carrie and her 5 friends equals 6 people that are dividing up 4 boxes. 4 boxes shared with 6 people is the same as 4 ÷ 6 = $^4/_6$ or $^2/_3$

$^4/_6$ ÷ $^2/_2$ = $^2/_3$ so they will each work on $^2/_3$ of a box.

10. Part A: 5 and 6

Part B: 5 $^1/_4$ pound. 8 friends share 42 pounds of coffee so divide up the coffee between 8 people: 42 ÷ 8 = 5 remainder 2, the remaining 2 pounds can be split between the 8 people 2 ÷ 8 = $^2/_8$ and simplified to $^1/_4$ so each person will get 5 $^1/_4$ pounds of coffee. The answer is between 5 and 6.

11. Part A: See explanation for pictures.

Part B: $^1/_3$ of the pizza. The picture should show 2 circles, each divided into 6 equal pieces. 2 pizzas divided by 6 people = 2 ÷ 6 = $^2/_6$ so each person will receive $^2/_6$ or $^1/_3$ of the pie.

$^2/_6$ ÷ $^2/_2$ = $^1/_3$

12. Part A: $^1/_2$ cup

Part B: 2 mini cakes . If 3 cups of flour is used to make 6 mini cakes, divide 3 cups by the 6 cakes: 3 ÷ 6 = $^3/_6$ or $^1/_2$

If 3 friends want to share the 6 cakes, divide the 6 cakes by the 3 friends: 6 ÷ 3 = 2 so they each take home 2 cakes.

5.NF.B.4, 5.NF.B.4.A, 5.NF.B.4.B Multiply Whole Numbers and Fractions

1. D. $^1/_3$ x 3 is the same as counting $^1/_3$ three times or thinking three groups of $^1/_3$. Count $^1/_3$ + $^1/_3$ + $^1/_3$ = $^3/_3$ or 1 whole.

2. A. Adding $^1/_4$ five times is the same as multiplying by $^1/_4$ x 5

3. B. 4 x $^2/_5$ or 4 groups of $^2/_5$ is the same as adding $^2/_5$ four times, which is shown in Choice B

4. C. Each of 3 pizzas has $^1/_6$ remaining so count $^1/_6$ + $^1/_6$ + $^1/_6$ or 3 x $^1/_6$ = $^3/_6$

5. B. 5 x $^4/_7$ is adding $^4/_7$ five times, which is the same as multiplying 4 x 5. The first step when multiplying a fraction and a whole number is to multiply the numerator times the fraction.

6. A. $^6/_8$ of the cake is leftover and of the leftovers $^1/_3$ has icing so multiply to find the remaining part with icing.

$^6/_8$ x $^1/_3$ = $^6/_{24}$ which can be reduced to $^1/_4$

7. D. $^3/_4$ x $^4/_5$ = $^{12}/_{20}$, 12 out of the 20 cubes are shaded blue

8. C. To find the area, multiply length x width

$^7/_8$ x $^5/_8$ = $^{35}/_{64}$

The model shows 8 by 8 square and 35 out of the 64 should be shaded to represent the area.

9. B. Multiply to find the fraction of students who have dogs.

$^2/_3$ x $^3/_4$ = $^6/_{12}$ which can be simplified to $^1/_2$

$^6/_{12}$ ÷ $^6/_6$ = $^1/_2$

10. Part A: $^4/_{20}$ x 80.

Part B: James scored 16 points during the game.

$^4/_{20}$ x 80 = (4 x 80) ÷ 20

4 x 80 = 320

320 ÷ 20 = 16

11. Yes. She is correct because a whole number times a fraction equals a number less than the whole number factor. 4 x $^1/_4$ = $^4/_4$ = 1

4 x $^5/_6$ = $^{20}/_6$ = 3 and $^2/_6$

When multiplying a whole number times a number less than 1 (fraction) the product is less than the whole number factor because you are counting repeated groups of fractions or numbers less than 1.

4 groups of $^1/_2$ = $^4/_2$ = 2

12. See explanation; $^{16}/_{30} \div ^2/_2 = ^8/_{15}$. To show $^4/_5 \times ^4/_6$ draw a 5 by 6 array. Share 4 columns vertically and 4 rows horizontally.

$^4/_5 \times ^4/_6 = 4 \times 4 = 16$

$5 \times 6 = 30$ so 16 out of the 30 squares should be shade. $^{16}/_{30}$ can be reduced to $^8/_{15}$ square feet.

5.NF.B.5 Interpret Multiplication as Scaling

1. B. The number line shows 4 scaled up 3 times to equal 12 which is the same as $3 \times 4 = 12$

2. C. The number line shows 3 scaled up 4 times to equal 12 which is the same as $4 \times 3 = 12$

3. A. $^1/_4 \times 5 = ^5/_4$, add $^1/_4$ 5 times

$^1/_4 + ^1/_4 + ^1/_4 + ^1/_4 + ^1/_4 = ^5/_4$

4. D. $^2/_3 \times 6 = ^{12}/_3$ which is the same as $12 \div 3 = 4$

4 is less than 6

so $^2/_3 \times 6 < 6$

5. B. $1 ^1/_2 \times 3$ means add $1 ^1/_2$ three times:

$1 ^1/_2 + 1 ^1/_2 + 1 ^1/_2 = 4 ^1/_2$

6. C. $13 \times ^8/_8 = 13$ so the product will be equal to 13.

$^8/_8$ equals 1 because $8 \div 8 = 1$ so $13 \times 1 = 13$.

7. A. $4 \times ^2/_5$ = a number less than 4

Add $^2/_5 + ^2/_5 + ^2/_5 + ^2/_5 = ^8/_5$

$8 \div 5 = 1$ R 3 so $^8/_5 = 1$ and $^3/_5$, which is less than 4.

8. B. The product will be greater than 5 because multiplying a mixed number and a whole number results in a larger number.

1 and $^4/_8 = ^{12}/_8$ as a improper fraction ($1 = ^8/_8 + ^4/_8 = ^{12}/_8$)

$^{12}/_8 \times 5 = ^{60}/_8$

$60 \div 8 = 7$ R $4 = 7 ^4/_8$

$7 ^4/_8$ or $7 ^1/_2$ is greater than the factor 5

9. D. A mixed number times a whole number will result in the largest product in this problem because multiplying whole numbers greater than 1 result in a product larger than the factors.

10. Robert is correct. Robert is correct because multiplying a whole number times a fraction will always result in a number smaller than the whole number. Counting a fraction is counting a part of a whole (a number less than 1) so the resulting product will be less than the original whole number factor.

Example: $^1/_2 \times 5 = ^5/_2$ or $2 ^1/_2$, which is less than 5.

11. Part A: The fraction must be an improper fraction in order to make the expression true.

Part B: Any regular fraction will work here – not improper fraction or mixed number.

Part C: Any regular fraction will work here – not improper fraction or mixed number.

Part D: See explanation.

Explanations will review a fraction times an improper fraction = a fraction larger than the original fraction.

A whole number times a fraction equals a number smaller than the whole number factor

An improper fraction (or mixed number) times a fraction equals a fraction smaller than the improper fraction.

12. less than < ; See explanation. A mixed number or improper fraction times a fraction equals a smaller fraction the mixed number. Counting a fraction of a number is counting part of a whole so the result will be less than the original number.

5.NF.B.6 Solve Word Problems Involving Multiplication of Fractions

1. C. If there are 25 students and $^2/_5$ are boys, multiply to find the number of boys out of the total amount. The fraction $^2/_5$ represents the portion of students that are boys.

2. A. Out of 112 tickets, $^3/_4$ are adult tickets. To find the number of adult tickets out of the total amount of tickets, multiply $112 \times ^3/_4$

$112 \times 3 = 336$

$336 \div 4 = 84$ tickets

3. D. The total amount of miles walked was $^9/_{12}$ and part of those miles was spent running. Multiply $^1/_6 \times ^9/_{12}$ to find the amount of miles ran.

4. B. One foot = 12 inches.

Her painting is $^3/_4$ of 12 inches long so multiply to find how long her painting is in inches.

$3 \times 12 = 36$

$36 \div 4 = 9$ inches

5. A. Multiply $^6/_8 \times ^4/_5$ to find the fraction of the painting that has stars.

$6 \times 4 = 24$

$8 \times 5 = 40$

$^{24}/_{40}$ can be simplified by 8

$24 \div 8 = 3$

$40 \div 8 = 5$ so $3/5$ of the painting has stars.

6. B. If she uses $5/8$ of the chocolate to make cookies and the rest to make brownies, to find the fraction of chocolate used to make brownies, subtract $8/8$ (whole amount) − $5/8 = 3/8$ so $3/8$ of the chocolate was used to make brownies. $3/8$ of $48 = 3/8 \times 48$

$48 \times 3 = 144$

$144 \div 8 = 18$ so 18 ounces was used to make brownies.

7. D. Kevin scores 30 points which is $1/3$ of the total amount because his teammates scored $2/3$ of the points. If $1/3 = 30$ points then add $30 + 30 = 60$ to find how many points the team scored as $2/3$ of the points $1/3 + 1/3 = 2/3$

8. C. $5/6$ of an hour means multiply by 60 since there are 60 minutes in 1 hour.

$5 \times 60 = 300$

$300 \div 6 = 50$ so it takes her 50 minutes to drive to her grandmother's house. If she drives there and back, add $50 + 50 = 100$ minutes total.

100 minutes can be changed into 1 hour 40 minutes because there are 60 minutes in 1 hour $100 - 60 = 40$

9. A. If the trip was $8\ 2/6$ hours total, multiply $2/5$ to find the amount of time spent on their break.

Change $8\ 2/6$ to an improper fraction: $6 \times 8 = 48 + 2 = 50$

$8\ 2/6 = 50/6$

Then multiply by $2/5$

$50/6 \times 2/5$

$50 \times 2 = 100$

$6 \times 5 = 30$

$100/30$ can be simplified to $10/3$ which is changed to a mixed number by dividing $10 \div 3 = 3$ R $1 = 3\ 1/3$ hours

10. $3\ 3/8$ were pepperoni pizzas. Multiply the total number of pizzas $4\ 1/2$ by $3/4$ to find the fraction of the pizzas that were pepperoni.

Change the mixed numbers to improper fractions to multiply:

$4\ 1/2 = 4 \times 2 = 8 + 1 = 9$

$4\ 1/2 = 9/2$

Multiply $9/2 \times 3/4$

$9 \times 3 = 27$

$2 \times 4 = 8$

Simplify $27/8$ to a mixed number

$27 \div 8 = 3$ R$3 = 3\ 3/8$ were pepperoni pizzas

11. Part A: Add the number of ounces the boys ate by changing $2/5$ to an equivalent fraction with a denominator of 10.

$2/5 \times 2/2 = 4/10$

Part B: $7/10$ ounces. $4/10 + 3/10 = 7/10$

Part C: 6 ounces remain. The boys ate $7/10$ of the bag so $3/10$ remains because $10/10$ (whole) − $7/10 = 3/10$

Multiply $3/10 \times 20$ to find how much remains.

$3 \times 20 = 60$

$60/10$ can be simplified: $60 \div 10 = 6$

12. Part A: 11 more ounces.

Subtract to find how many more ounces: $5/6 - 3/8$, change the fractions to equivalent fraction with a denominator of 24

$5/6 \times 4/4 = 20/24$

$3/8 \times 3/3 = 9/24$

$20 - 9 = 11$ ounces

Part B: 16 ounces remaining. If Nathan drank $1/3$ of the 24 ounces, he has $2/3$ of the water remaining. $2/3 \times 24 = 48 \div 3 = 16$, he has 16 ounces remaining.

Part C: 35 ounces remain altogether. Charlie drank $3/8$ so $5/8$ of the water is left in the bottle. $5/8 \times 24 = 5 \times 24 = 120$, $120 \div 8 = 15$ ounces.

Anthony drank $5/6$ so $1/6$ remains. $1/6 \times 24 = 1 \times 24 = 24$, $24 \div 6 = 4$, so 4 ounces remain. Add the remaining amounts: $16 + 15 + 4 = 35$ ounces remain altogether.

5.NF.B.7, 5 NF.B.7.A, 5 NF.B.7.B, Solve Word Problems Involving Division of Fractions

1. B. 2 pizzas divided into $1/3$ sized slices = $2 \div 1/3$ = 6 slices. If the pizza is cut into thirds, there will be 6 pieces of pizza.

2. A. 4 feet divided into $1/4$ sized pieces = $4 \div 1/4$ = $4 \times 4 = 16$ pieces.

3. D. 3 pizzas cut into sixths is $3 \div 1/6 = 3 \times 6 = 18$ pieces.

4. C. 6 pieces of paper cut into $1/5$ sized pieces is $6 \div 1/5 = 6 \times 5 = 30$ pieces of paper.

5. A. 3 cups of water fills $1/4$ of the bucket so $3 \times 4 = 12$ cups of water total in the bucket.

6. B. $1/3$ of the cake divided by 2 people means

split the remaining third into 2 pieces. $1/3 \div 2 = 1/6$ because the third is now cut into 2 pieces which represents sixths size pieces of the entire tray of brownies.

7. C. $1/2$ pound divided into 8 bags = $1/2 \div 8 = 1/2 \times 1/8 = 1/16$

Cut the $1/2$ pound bag into 8 parts and each part represents $1/16$ of the whole bag.

8. D. Kellen spends $5/6$ of his money so $1/6$ remains: $6/6 - 5/6 = 1/6$

$1/6$ of his money divided into 2 piggy banks: $1/6 \div 2 = 1/6 \times 1/2 = 1/12$ so $1/12$ of his birthday money is put into the 2 piggy banks.

9. A. If half of her day is spent cleaning each of 5 rooms for the same amount of time, divide $1/2 \div 5 = 1/2 \times 1/5 = 1/10$ of her day is spent cleaning each room.

10. See explanation for picture; 16 guests. 4 cakes divided into $1/4$ = 16 pieces so she can share with 16 guests.

$4 \div 1/4 = 4 \times 4 = 16$

Drawing should be 4 shapes for a cake (square, circle, etc.) and each cake is split into 4 equal pieces so there are 16 pieces total.

11. Part A: 6 cakes. 2 cups of oil ÷ $1/3$ cup of oil for each cake = 6 cakes. $2 \div 1/3 = 2 \times 3 = 6$ cakes

Part B: 8 cakes. 4 cups of apples ÷ $1/2$ cup of apples for each cake = 8 cakes. $4 \div 1/2 = 4 \times 2 = 8$ cakes

Part C: 12 cakes. 3 cups of milk ÷ $1/4$ cup of milk for each cake = 12 cakes. $3 \div 1/4 = 3 \times 4 = 12$ cakes

Part D: 6 cakes. She only has enough oil for 6 cakes, so she can only make 6 cakes.

12. Part A: $1/18$ in each glass

$1/6$ of the orange juice divided into 3 glasses: $1/6 \div 3 = 1/6 \times 1/3 = 1/18$ in each glass

Part B: $1/8$ of the orange juice is in each of the 4 smaller glasses.

Change $1/3$ to a denominator of 6.

$1/3 \times 2/2 = 2/6$, so the $2/6$ that Sandra poured for herself + $1/6$ she already poured = $3/6$ of the orange juice is no longer in the pitcher which means $3/6$ remains in the pitcher.

$3/6$ remaining divided into 4 glasses is $3/6 \div 4 = 3/6 \times 1/4 = 3/24$, which can be simplified into $1/8$

$3/24 \div 3/3 = 1/8$ of the orange juice is in each of the 4 smaller glasses.

MEASUREMENT AND DATA
5.MD.A.1 Convert Units of Measurement

1. B. Convert 25 cm to mm.

1 cm = 10 mm so multiply by 10

25 x 10 = 250 mm

2. D. $1/3$ of a foot = $1/3 \times 12$ inches (12 inches in 1 foot)

1 x 12 = 12

$12/3 = 12 \div 3 = 4$ inches

3. A. $2/3$ of an hour = $2/3 \times 60$ minutes

2 x 60 = 120

$1\ 20/3 = 120 \div 3 = 40$ minutes

4. C. 1.56 meters = 456 centimeters

1 meter = 100 cm so multiply by 100

4.56 x 100 = 456 cm

5. A. $1/5$ divided into 4 cups = $1/5 \div 4 = 1/5 \times 1/4 = 1/20$ liters of the tea is in each of the 4 cups.

There are 1000 ml in 1 liter so multiply $1/20$ times 1000 to find the amount of milliliters in each cup:

$1/20$ of 1000 ml = $1/20 \times 1000 = 1000/20 = 1000 \div 20 = 50$ milliliters.

6. B. 2 pounds of cherries split into 4 tarts means divide 2 pounds by 4 tarts = $2 \div 4 = 2/4$ or $1/2$ pound of cherries are in each tart. There are 16 ounces in 1 pound so multiply $1/2 \times 16$ to find how many ounces are in each tart. $1/2 \times 16 = 16/2 = 8$ ounces of cherries in each tart.

7. D. 24 ounces in half the bottle means add 24 + 24 to find how many ounces are in the whole bottle: 48 ounces

48 ounces changed to cups:

8 ounces = 1 cup so divide 48 by 8 to find the number of cups in 48 ounces.

$48 \div 8 = 6$ cups.

8. B. 5 yards cut into 6 pieces means divide $5 \div 6 = 5/6$ yard for each piece. There are 36 inches in 1 yard to multiply $5/6 \times 36$ to find the number of inches in $5/6$ of a yard.

$5/6 \times 36 = 5 \times 36 = 180$; $180/6 = 180 \div 6 = 30$ inches

9. A. 5 tigers weight $1/2$ of a ton. 1 ton = 2000 pounds so $1/2$ ton means divide by 2: $2000 \div 2 = 1000$ so 5 tigers weigh 1000 pounds. Divide to find the weight of each tiger.

$1000 \div 5 = 200$ so each tiger weighs 200 pounds.

10. **1.68 meters.**

1680 millimeters. 1 cm = 10 mm

100 cm = 1 m

To convert 168 cm to meters, divide by 100 since there are 100 cm in 1 m

168 ÷ 100 = 1.68 meters

To convert 168 cm to millimeters, multiply by 10 since there are 10 mm in 1 cm, 168 x 10 = 1680 millimeters.

11. Part A.   14 ounces of grapes

Part B. 4 ounces of blueberries

Part C. Strawberries.

1 pound = 16 ounces

Grapes:

Multiply ⁷/₈ by 16 ounces to find the number of ounces in ⁷/₈ pound

⁷/₈ x 16 = 7 x 16 = 112

1 ¹²/₈ = 112 ÷ 8 = 14 ounces

Blueberries:

Multiply ¹/₄ by 16 ounces to find the number of ounces in ¹/₄ pound.

¹/₄ x 16 = 1 x 16 = 16

¹⁶/₄ = 4 ounces

There are 16 ounces in 1 pound and 8 ounces in ¹/₂ pound (8 + 8 = 16).

1 ¹/₂ pounds = 16 ounces in 1 pound + 8 ounces in ¹/₂ pound = 16 + 8 = 24 ounces of strawberries. So Monica bought more strawberries than grapes.

12. 25 gallons for the fence. He uses 220 quarts total and uses 20 extra quarts for the garage so subtract 220-20 to find the quarts used for the garage and fence, 220 - 20 = 200, so 200 quarts are divided evenly between the garage and fence.

Divide 200 by 4 to find how many gallons are in 200 quarts because there are 4 quarts in 1 gallon, 200 ÷ 4 = 50 gallons used to paint the garage and fence.

To find the gallons used for the fence, divide 50 by 2 to split the amount of paint between the garage and fence: 50 ÷ 2 = 25 gallons for each.

5.MD.A.2 Display Data in Line Plots & Solve Problems Using Line Plots

1. B. 4 days recorded in October have ¹/₈ inch of rainfall, which was the most frequent amount.

2. A. It did not rain for 2 days because there are 2 raindrops above the zero inch recording.

3. D. Add the fractions based on the number of raindrops at each fraction: ¹/₈ + ¹/₈ + ¹/₈ + ¹/₈ + ¹/₄ + ¹/₄ + ¹/₄ + ¹/₂ + ¹/₂ + ¹/₂ + ³/₄ + 1 =

⁴/₈ + ³/₄ + 1 ¹/₂ + ³/₄ + 1 = 4 ¹/₂ inches total rainfall.

4. C. The longest length of ribbon is 2 ¹/₄ foot since that is the largest fraction on the line plot.

5. B. Jamie has 5 ribbons that are 1 ¹/₂ inches long, which is the most frequent length recorded.

6. A. Add the fractional amounts according to the number of ribbons for each length 25 feet.

1 x 2 = 2

3 x 1 ¹/₄ = 3 ³/₄

5 x 1 ¹/₂ = 7 ¹/₂

3 x 1 ³/₄ = 5 ¹/₄

2 x 1 = 2

2 x 2 ¹/₄ = 4 ¹/₂

Add the products of each ribbon length:

2 + 3 ³/₄ + 7 ¹/₂ + 5 ¹/₄ + 2 + 4 ¹/₂ = 25 feet.

7. See line plot below.

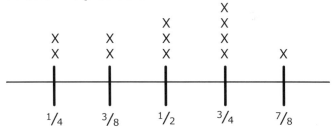

Length of Cherries Picked (inches)

8. D. Add the number of Xs at ¹/₂ inch, ³/₈ inch and ¹/₄ inch:

2 + 2 + 3 = 7, so 7 cherries are ¹/₂ inch in length or less

9. A. There are 3 cherries that are ¹/₂ inch long and 1 cherry that is ⁷/₈ inch long so subtract 3 - 1 = 2 cherries

10. C. Find the total length of the cherries by adding the length of the each cherry which equals 6 ⁵/₈, the subtract 7 - 6 ⁵/₈ = ³/₈, so ³/₈ inch in length is needed to have a sum of 7 inches for the total length of cherries.

11. See line plot below.

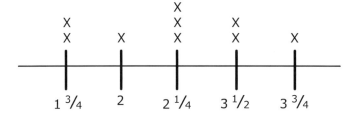

Distance Run in PE Class in Miles

12. 2 5/9 miles. First, find the total distance run by adding the distances in the chart, which equals 23 miles: $1\frac{3}{4} + 1\frac{3}{4} + 2 + 2\frac{1}{4} + 2\frac{1}{4} + 2\frac{1}{4} + 3\frac{1}{2} + 3\frac{1}{2} + 3\frac{3}{4} = 23$

To find the average, divide the total amount of miles by the number of students that ran in PE class: $23 \div 9 = 2$ R 5 so $2\frac{5}{9}$ miles was the average amount ran during class.

5.MD.C.3, 5 MD.C.3.A, 5 MD.C.3.B Recognize & Understand Volume

1. B. Counting the blocks Kelly used, there are 6 cubes in the rectangle so the shape has a volume of 6 cubic inches.

2. C. She uses 4 cubes to make a square so the volume of her shape will be 4 cubic inches.

3. A. There are 9 cubes in the shape so the volume is 9 cubic inches.

4. D. The bottom layer of this shape has 4 cubes, with another 2 cubes in the top layer so there are 6 cubes total in this shape = volume of 6 cubic inches.

5. A. The bottom layer has 5 cubes and the second layer has 5 cubes so the total number of cubes is 5 + 5 = 10 cubic inches.

6. C. The front layer of this shape is 6 cubic inches and the back layer is 6 cubic inches so 6 + 6 = 12 cubic inches total.

7. B. A 4 inch by 5 inch rectangle means there will be 4 rows of 5 cubes in each row, making an array of 20 cubes. The volume will be 20 cubic inches.

8. D. Count the bottom layer which is 2 cubes by 3 cubes= 6 cubes. The top layer has 2 cubes so 6 + 2 = 8 cubic inches.

9. C. The bottom layer is 6 cubic inches, the middle layer is 5, and the top layer is half of the bottom (6 ÷ 2 = 3) 3. Add 6 + 5 + 3 = 14 cubic inches.

10. Answers may vary. The 2 shapes must be different but have the same volume of 12 cubic inches using the dot-to-dot as 1 cubic unit.

11. Volume = 5 cubic inches. The bottom layer of the shape has 4 cubes even though the one cube is hidden under the top cube. 4 + 1 on top = 5 cubic inches.

12. Volume= 10 cubic inches. The bottom layer has 5 cubes with one cube being hidden under the top layer. The top layer already has 1 cube and then add 4 more to cover the bottom layer: 5 + 1 + 4 = 10 cubic inches.

5.MD.C.4 Measure Volume by Counting Cubes

1. B. The top row is 2 by 5 array which equals 2 x 5 = 10 cubes. The 2 rows are the same, so 2 x 5 x 2 = volume = 20

2. A. The first horizontal layer is a 4 by 3 array = 4 x 3 = 12. The second horizontal layer is the same 4 x 3 array so 12 + 12 = 24

3. C. Counting horizontally, there are 4 layers with 6 cubes in each layer.

4. B. The bottom layer is shaded, which is 4 cubes. The side flaps show the box will have a height of 1 inch so 4 x 1 = 4 cubes will fit in the box.

5. D. The base layer is 24 cubes and the box is 3 layers tall so multiply 24 x 3 = 72 cubic inches.

6. A. The base layer is 2 cubes by 3 cubes = 2 x 3 = 6 cubes. The figure is 4 cubes tall so multiply 4 x 6 = 24 cubic inches.

7. C. The base layer is 12 cubes and the side flaps show the first row would be the side of the 1st layer and the 2nd row on the flap shows a 2nd layer: 12 + 12 = 24 cubes would fill the box.

8. B. The outer layer is 7 cubes and the top layer is 5 cubes. Double the top layer since there is the same amount of cubes in under the top layer: 5 + 5 + 7 =17 cubic units.

9. D. The bottom layer is 4 cubes by 5 cubes = 4 x 5 = 20

The next set is 2 layers of 4 by 3 cubes = 4 x 3 = 12 + 12 = 24

The top layer is 8 cubes.

Add all the layers; 8 + 24 + 20 = 52 cubic units.

10. Answer will vary. The 2 layers should add up to 36 using the dot-to-dot as one cubic unit.

11. Volume = 48 cubic units. The bottom layer of this figure is 4 x 4 = 16 cubes. The flap shows the box is 3 layers tall so 16 x 3 = 48 cubic units.

12. Volume = 50 cubic units. The bottom horizontal layer is 16 cubes and the next layer is the same amount – 16 cubes so 16 + 16 = 32.

The 3rd layer from the bottom is 11 cubes.

The top layer is 7 cubes. Add the layers: 16 + 16 + 11 + 7 = 50 cubic units.

5.MD.C.5, 5.MD.C.5.A, 5.MD.C.5.B, 5.MD.C.5.C, Solve Problems Involving Volume

1. C. Multiply the length x width x height to find the

volume of rectangular prisms: 4 x 3 x 3 = 36 cubic inches.

2. A. Multiply the length x width x height to find the volume of rectangular prisms: 5 x 7 x 3 =

3. B. Multiply the length x width x height to find the volume of rectangular prisms: 8 x 4 x 2 = 64

4. D. Multiply the area of the layers by 3 because there are 3 layers each with an area of 14 sq. ft. = 14 x 3 = 42 cu. feet.

5. A. The area = length x width so the only remaining computation is multiply the area x 12 the height:

20 x 12 = 240

6. C. If the length is double the width, take the width and double it or multiply by 2: 2 x 2 =4 so the length is 4

Multiply the length x width x height = 3 x 4 x 2 = 24

7. B. A cube has all sides the same length, so multiply 6 x 6 x 6 = 216 to find the volume.

8. D. Use the formula for volume to solve: 6 x 3 x n = 72

18 x n = 72, to find n, use division to solve: 72 ÷ 18 = 4 so the missing height is 4 feet.

9. A. The smaller bottom rectangle has a dimensions of 5 x 2 x 2 = 20. If the total height of the left side of the figure is 4 inches, then divide by 2 to split the measurement across the top and bottom figure. 4 ÷ 2 = 2 so the height of each rectangular prism is 2 inches.

The larger rectangle has a length of 13, width of 2 and height of 2. 13 x 2 x 2 = 52

Add the volumes of the 2 rectangles: 52+ 20 = 72 cubic inches.

10. 528 square inches. First subtract 26 -15 to find the height of the tank that is not filled with water. 26- 15 = 11 inches. Multiply the area of the base (l x w) by the remaining height to find the volume needed to fill the tank: 11 x 48 = 528 square inches.

11. Answers will vary. Length x width x height must equal 360

Possible dimensions include:

6 x 6 x 10   12 x 3 x 10

12 x 5 x 6   18 x 2 x 10

9 x 4 x 10

12. See explanation. Half of 160 is 80 because 160 ÷ 2 = 80. The dimensions of Nicole's rectangle could be 4 x 2 x 10

No, Sarah should not double the dimensions of her rectangle to double the volume: Her current rectangular prism is 160 sq.in. The dimensions could be 4 x 4 x 10 = 160. If she doubles the dimensions: 8 x 8 x 20, the volume would be 1,280 which is not double 160. 160 doubled is 160 x 2 = 320

13. See explanation. Find out volume of the box by multipying 12 x 9 x 6 = 648 cubic inches. Then, calculate the volume of one block, which is 3 x 3 x 3 = 27 cubic inches. In order to find out how many blocks fit in the box, divide 648 by 27 = 24 blocks.

GEOMETRY

5.G.A.1 Understand Graph Points on the Coordinate Plane

1. D. The point is located at 1 $^3/_4$ because the number line is divided into 4 equal parts between the whole numbers and point A is located at 1 $^3/_4$

2. A. Point B is located at 3 $^1/_3$. The number line is divided into 3 equal parts or thirds between the whole numbers.

3. C. The first coordinate for the pentagon is on the X-axis: located at 8.

4. B. The square is located at (1, 6) and 6 is the location of the square on the Y-axis.

5. B. The arrow is located at (3, 4). The arrow is located on the 3 on the X-axis and 4 on the Y-axis.

6. C. On the X-axis, the smiley face is located 4 units from the origin zero.

7. A. The star is located on the 2 on the X-axis and 3 on the Y-axis so the point is labeled as (2, 3).

8. D. The star and the heart are both located at 2 on the X-axis.

9. C. The smiley face and star are both located at the 3 on the Y-axis.

10.

The triangle: (9, 8)

The heart: (2, 0)

The pentagon: (8, 1)

11. No. No she is incorrect. The smiley face is located at 4 on the X-axis and 3 on the Y-axis, so the coordinate for the smiley face is (4, 3). (3, 4) is another point on the grid, the arrow – located at the 3 on the X-axis and 3 on the Y-axis. She cannot use both (4, 3) and (3, 4) interchangeably since they represent different locations on the grid.

12. Arrow and the square. Coordinates of arrow: **(3, 4)**; Coordinates of square: **(1, 6)**

Square and triangle. Coordinates of square: **(1, 6)**; Coordinates of triangle: **(9, 8)**

5.G.A.2 Solve Problems Using Coordinate Plane

1. B. (3,2) is a coordinate that is on the line DZ. The line is located at 3 units on the X-axis and 2 units on the Y-axis.

2. D. 6 on the X-axis and 7 on the Y-axis is not on line DZ, the coordinate (6, 7) is above the line.

3. A. X – 1 = y fits this line because each coordinate on the line has a value of y that is one less than x. Example: (2, 1), (3, 2), (4, 3) and so on.

4. C. In the ordered pair (4, 10) 4 is the x-coordinate and 10 is the y-coordinate, so double x (4 x 2 = 8) and halve y (10 ÷ 2 = 5), so the resulting ordered pair is (8, 5).

5. B. The intersecting point on two lines is (3, 1½) with 3 on the x-axis and 1 ½ on the y-axis.

6. D. 4 on the x-axis and 3 ½ on the y-axis is a point on line QU

7. A. The x-coordinates on the line RM are 1 ½ units larger than the y-coordinate, so the rule is x – 1 ½ = y

Example (2, ½):
2 – 1 ½ = ½

8. C. The point (1, ½) fits the rule x – ½ = y
1 – ½ = ½ so the rule for a line parallel to RM is x – ½ = y

9. D. The y-coordinate 3 is 1 ½ units larger than the x-coordinate so the rule x + 1 ½ = y fits the ordered pairs (1 ½, 3) and (3, 4 ½).

10. See below.

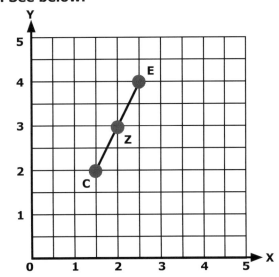

11. Answers will vary. The ordered pairs must follow the rule X x 2 = Y *(x times 2 = y)*.

If y is double x, then x times 2 = y

12. Answers will vary. The line must pass through (1 ½, 3) and follow the rule x + 1 ½ = y

5.G.B.3 Understand Attributes of Two-Dimensional Shapes

1. B. The definition of a square (4 right angles, 4 sides equal length) fits the definition of a rectangle (4 right angles, opposite sides parallel and congruent).

2. A. The sum of the interior angles in a triangle equals 180 degrees so a right triangle has one angle that is 90° and the other 2 angles must be less than 90° to equal a total of 180 degrees.

3. C. A scalene triangle has all sides with different lengths and therefore all angles will be different measures.

4. D. A trapezoid cannot be a square because the definition of a trapezoid states it only has 1 set of parallel sides and a squares has 2 sets of parallel sides.

5. A. In a regular hexagon, all sides are congruent and therefore all angle measures are congruent so A is false.

6. B. The polygon is a quadrilateral because it has 4 sides, a parallelogram because opposite sides are parallel and a rhombus because all 4 sides are the same length with 2 acute and 2 obtuse angles.

7. A. A trapezoid has 4 sides and one 1 pair of parallel sides. It can also have 2 right angles.

8. C. The 2 base angles are congruent and the 2 legs on the trapezoid are also congruent in an isosceles trapezoid.

9. D. If a parallelogram has 4 right angles and opposite sides parallel, then it can be called a rectangle.

10. See explanation. At least 1 pair of parallel sides: trapezoid, rhombus.

At least 1 right angle: right triangle.

Both: rectangle, square.

11. See below.

Part A: Rhombus:

Part B: Rhombus with 4 right angles:

a. Square

Part C: Rectangle:

Part D: Rectangle with 4 congruent sides:

a. Square

12. Yes. Kim is correct. In number 11, you can see a rhombus must have 4 sides of equal length but not necessarily any right angles. A rectangle must have 4 right angles but not necessarily 4 sides of equal length. A rectangle and rhombus are not by definition a square because a square must always have 4 congruent sides and 4 right angles, but a square is always a rhombus or rectangle.

5.G.B.4 Classify Two-Dimensional Shapes

1. D. A regular pentagon has 5 sides of equal length and does not have any parallel sides.

2. C. A scalene triangle has 3 sides that are all different lengths.

3. B. The rhombus has 4 sides of equal length and no right angles.

4. A. A square has 4 sides of equal length, an equilateral triangle has 3 sides of equal length, and a regular octagon has 8 sides of equal length

5. D. Each shape has at last 1 right angle, the right triangle, pentagon and trapezoid.

6. A. Isosceles triangles have 2 sides that are the same. As this triangle has 2 sides that are 12 feet, it is an isosceles triangle.

7. B. A trapezoid can have sides of varying lengths but must have 1 set of parallel sides.

8. C. A parallelogram has 2 sets of opposite angles that are the same measure.

9. D. A rhombus has 4 sides of equal length so divide the perimeter by 4 to find the length of each side: 212 ÷ 4 = 53

10. Answers may vary. All sides must be the same length in cm or inches.

11. B. Possibly lengths and heights:

4 x 6 inches

8 x 3 inches

2 x 12 inches

1 x 24 inches

12. Answers may vary. Isosceles trapezoid has 2 opposite sides that are the same length. So the measurement of the opposite sides will be the same length, therefore it meets the definition of an isosceles trapezoid.

NY STANDARDS ASSESSMENT
PRACTICE TESTS

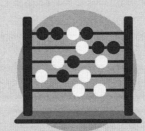

NY STANDARDS ASSESSMENT

Mathematics Practice Test One Session One

1. What is the distance of point R from the origin zero?

- Ⓐ 3 1/3
- Ⓑ 3 2/3
- Ⓒ 3
- Ⓓ 3 3/4

2. What is the last step in this equation?

$$31 + (14 - 2 \times 3) \times 2$$

- Ⓐ (14 − 2 x 3)
- Ⓑ 31 x 2
- Ⓒ 31 + 16
- Ⓓ 8 x 2

3. What is the sum of 1/3 + 1/6 ?

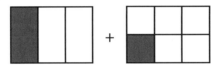

- Ⓐ 2/3
- Ⓑ 2/6
- Ⓒ 3/6
- Ⓓ 4/6

4. Jenna has 1/100 the amount of LEGOs as Tommy. Tommy has 4,300 LEGOs. How many LEGOs does Jenna have?

- Ⓐ 43
- Ⓑ 430
- Ⓒ 100
- Ⓓ 4

5. Use the coordinate grid below to answer questions A and B.

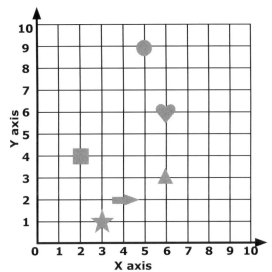

Which shapes are exactly 2 units away from each other on the X-axis and 8 units away from each other on the y-axis?

    Ⓐ Arrow and Star

    Ⓑ Star and Circle

    Ⓒ Square and Heart

    Ⓓ Heart and Triangle

6. Brinkley, Aaron, and Calvin share 5 pizzas. What fraction of the pizzas will each friend receive? Use the diagram to help you choose the correct answer.

    Ⓐ $3 \div 5 = 3/5$

    Ⓑ $3 \div 5 = 3/3$

    Ⓒ $5 \div 3 = 1\ 2/3$

    Ⓓ $5 \div 3 = 1\ 3/5$

7. Cassandra has 0.6 of a lasagna leftover from her party to share with her friends the next day. If she splits the lasagna into 0.2 size pieces, which equation shows how many pieces of lasagna she has?

    Ⓐ $0.6 \div 0.2 = 3$

    Ⓑ $0.6 \times 0.2 = 0.12$

    Ⓒ $0.2 \div 0.6 = 0.12$

    Ⓓ $0.6 \div 0.2 = 0.3$

8. Mrs. Mason spends half of her day on Saturday running errands. If she goes to 8 stores, each for the same amount of time, what fraction of her day is spent in each store?
   - Ⓐ $1/24$ of her day is spent in each store
   - Ⓑ $1/4$ of her day is spent in each store
   - Ⓒ $1/8$ of her day is spent in each store
   - Ⓓ $1/16$ of her day is spent in each store

9. Joey solved his math problem by moving the decimal point 3 places to the right as shown.

   $$4.823 \longrightarrow 4,823$$

   Which of the descriptions explains how Joey got her answer?
   - Ⓐ He divided 4.823 by 100
   - Ⓑ He multiplied 4.823 by 100
   - Ⓒ He divided 4.823 by 1,000
   - Ⓓ He multiplied 4.823 by 10^3

10. Which statement is true about $4 \times 2/5$?
    - Ⓐ The product will be less than 4.
    - Ⓑ The product will be greater than 4.
    - Ⓒ The product will be equal to 4.
    - Ⓓ The product will be less than $2/5$.

11. Santo's keychain is $1/4$ of a foot long. How many inches long is the keychain?
    - Ⓐ 6 inches
    - Ⓑ 3 inches
    - Ⓒ 5 inches
    - Ⓓ 4 inches

12. Kevin has a rectangular prism that measures 6 inches by 12 inches by 8 inches. Carlos' prism has a volume that is $1/3$ of Kevin's prism. What could be the dimensions of Carlos' prism?

- Ⓐ 8 x 5 x 5
- Ⓑ 8 x 9 x 3
- Ⓒ 7 x 6 x 5
- Ⓓ 6 x 8 x 4

13. What is the volume of this box when it's completely full with 1-inch cubes? The box has a height of 7 inches.

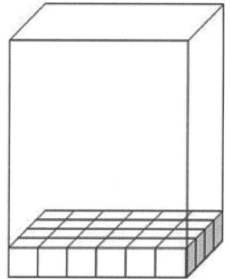

Ⓐ 42 cubic inches
Ⓑ 168 cubic inches
Ⓒ 28 cubic inches
Ⓓ 170 cubic inches

14. Jerry walks $9/10$ of a mile every day. This time, he decides to jog for $1/4$ of the time. What part of a mile does he run? Choose the equation needed to solve.

Ⓐ $9/10 + 1/4 =$
Ⓑ $9/10 - 1/4 =$
Ⓒ $9/10 \div 1/4 =$
Ⓓ $9/10 \times 1/4 =$

15. Which statement describes how to find the volume of this rectangular prism?

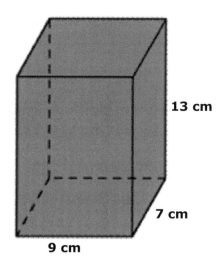

Ⓐ Add the length, width and height.
Ⓑ Add the length and width, then multiply by the height.
Ⓒ Determine the area of the base, then multiply by the height.
Ⓓ Determine the area of the base, then add height.

PRACTICE TEST ONE

16. What is the volume of this figure in cubic units?

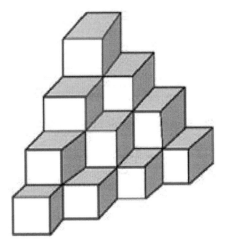

Ⓐ 10 cubic units
Ⓑ 16 cubic units
Ⓒ 18 cubic units
Ⓓ 20 cubic units

17. Which of the polygons below have 4 congruent sides?

trapezoid

rhombus

parallelogram

square

Ⓐ rhombus and square
Ⓑ rhombus and trapezoid
Ⓒ parallelogram and square
Ⓓ parallelogram and trapezoid

18. Use the number line to find ¹⁄₄ scaled up 6 times.

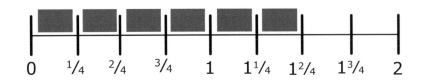

Ⓐ ¹⁄₄ x 6 = ⁶⁄₄
Ⓑ ¹⁄₄ x 6 = ⁴⁄₄
Ⓒ ¹⁄₄ + 6 = ⁶⁄₄
Ⓓ ¹⁄₄ - 6 = ⁶⁄₄

19. Which value below is the largest?

    Ⓐ seventy-nine and 3 hundreths

    Ⓑ (7 x 10) + (9 x $\frac{1}{10}$) + (5 x $\frac{1}{100}$)

    Ⓒ (7 x 10) + (4 x 1) + (7 x $\frac{1}{10}$) + (8 x $\frac{1}{100}$)

    Ⓓ 78.582

20. Which statement below about quadrilaterals is true?

    Ⓐ A rhombus is also a parallelogram

    Ⓑ A square is not a rhombus

    Ⓒ A rectangle is not a quadrilateral

    Ⓓ A trapezoid is also a square

21. What is the next set of numbers in this pattern?

    x: 23, 18, 20, 15, 17, 12, 14
    y: 7, 11, 14, 18, 21, 25, 28

    Ⓐ x = 32, y = 9 (32,9)

    Ⓑ x = 16, y = 31 (16, 31)

    Ⓒ x = 10, y = 34 (10, 34)

    Ⓓ x = 9, y = 32 (9, 32)

22. Marco made 7 trays with 6 cookies in each tray. He kept 10 cookies for himself and gave 4 cookies to each of his friends. Write an expression that can be used to find the number of friends with whom Marco shared cookies.

    Ⓐ 10 + 4 ÷ 6 = x

    Ⓑ [(7 + 6) - 4] + 10 = 17

    Ⓒ [(7 x 6) − 10] ÷ 4 = 8

    Ⓓ [(7 x 6) + 10] ÷ 4 = 13

23. Which equation shows one way to solve 4 x $\frac{2}{5}$?

    Ⓐ $\frac{2}{5}$ + $\frac{2}{5}$ + $\frac{2}{5}$ =

    Ⓑ $\frac{2}{5}$ + $\frac{2}{5}$ + $\frac{2}{5}$ + $\frac{2}{5}$ =

    Ⓒ $\frac{4}{5}$ + $\frac{4}{5}$ + $\frac{4}{5}$ + $\frac{4}{5}$ =

    Ⓓ $\frac{2}{5}$ + $\frac{2}{5}$ + $\frac{2}{5}$ + $\frac{2}{5}$ + $\frac{2}{5}$ =

24. Carol has 4 1/7 feet of floral wrapping paper and 3 6/8 feet of Christmas wrapping paper, and 4 4/9 feet of birthday wrapping paper. Rounded to the nearest half foot, about how many feet of wrapping paper does Carol have?
- (A) 13 1/2 feet.
- (B) 12 1/2 feet.
- (C) 11 1/2 feet.
- (D) 4 1/2 feet.

25. Which decimal below would be rounded to 58.6?
- (A) 57.68
- (B) 58.63
- (C) 58.54
- (D) 58.67

26. Corey has a bottle of juice that is one-third of the way full with 16 ounces. How many cups are in the entire bottle of juice?
- (A) 5 cups
- (B) 3 cups
- (C) 8 cups
- (D) 6 cups

27. Mrs. Dema has 6/8 of a tray of cookies leftover from her party. Of the leftover cookies, 1/4 of them have nuts. What fraction of the leftover cookies do not have nuts? Choose the equation needed to solve this problem.
- (A) 6/8 x 3/4 =
- (B) 6/8 ÷ 1/4 =
- (C) 6/8 − 1/4 =
- (D) 6/8 + 3/4 =

28. Gino folds the figure to make a box and fills the box with 1-centimeter cubes. The shaded cubes represent the bottom of the box. How many cubes will fill the box?

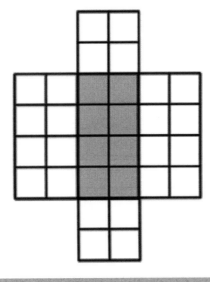

- (A) 16 cubes
- (B) 20 cubes
- (C) 12 cubes
- (D) 10 cubes

29. Samantha has a pitcher of water. She pours $1/2$ of the water into a water bottle. Then she pours $1/2$ of the remaining water for herself and then pours the water remaining in the pitcher into 4 glasses. How much of the water is in each glass?
    - (A) $1/4$ of the original water is in each glass
    - (B) $2/1$ of the original water is in each glass
    - (C) $1/16$ of the original water is in each glass
    - (D) $1/2$ of the original water is in each glass

30. Mr. Harold buys 5 sets of 25 stickers. He gives 4 stickers to each of his 20 students. How many stickers does he have left? Which expression can be used to solve this problem?
    - (A) 25 x 5 − (20 + 4)
    - (B) (5 x 25) − (4 x 20)
    - (C) (5 x 25) − 24
    - (D) (4 x 20) + 5 x 25

Session Two

31. The line plot below shows the length of different pieces of yarn Kelly uses for knitting.

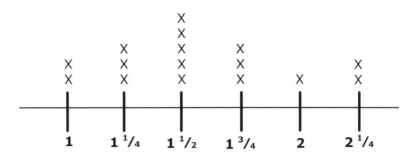

Length of Yarn (feet)

How many more feet of yarn does she need to have a total of 30 $^1/_2$ feet of yarn?

Ⓐ 5 $^1/_2$ feet

Ⓑ 5 $^3/_4$ feet

Ⓒ 6 $^1/_2$ feet

Ⓓ 5 feet

32. The perimeter of a square is 232 inches. What is the length of one side?

Ⓐ 29 inches

Ⓑ 58 inches

Ⓒ 4 inches

Ⓓ 52 inches

33. Jerry bought potting soil for his garden. He uses 1 $^2/_8$ kg of soil for the roses, 2 $^1/_3$ kg for the shrubs and $^4/_6$ kg for his flowers. In simplest form, how many kilograms of potting soil did Jerry use?

Ⓐ 4 $^8/_{24}$ kg

Ⓑ 3 $^1/_4$ kg

Ⓒ 4 $^9/_{24}$ kg

Ⓓ 4 $^1/_4$ kg

34. Choose the terms that describe this polygon.

Ⓐ parallelogram, quadrilateral, square
Ⓑ quadrilateral, parallelogram, polygon
Ⓒ rhombus, quadrilateral, parallelogram
Ⓓ rectangle, rhombus, parallelogram

PRACTICE TEST ONE

35. What is the rule for a line that contains the points (1 $\frac{1}{3}$, 3 $\frac{2}{3}$) and (5, 7 $\frac{1}{3}$)?

   Ⓐ x − 2 $\frac{1}{3}$ = y

   Ⓑ x + 2 $\frac{2}{3}$ = y

   Ⓒ x + $\frac{1}{3}$ = y

   Ⓓ x + 2 $\frac{1}{3}$ = y

36. Macey is solving a volume problem, but she already knows the volume is 108 cubic inches. The length of the figure is 6 inches and the width of the figure half the length in inches. What is the height of the shape?

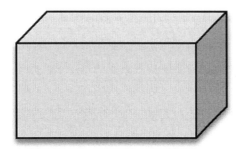

   Ⓐ 6 inches
   Ⓑ 5 inches
   Ⓒ 3 inches
   Ⓓ 4 inches

37. Charlie is cutting craft ribbon for an art project. He has 510 centimeters of ribbon and needs 42 separate pieces of ribbon, all the same length, with no ribbon left over. How long will each ribbon be in centimeters?

   Ⓐ 12 and $\frac{1}{7}$ cm long

   Ⓑ 11 and $\frac{1}{7}$ cm long

   Ⓒ 12 and $\frac{1}{8}$ cm long

   Ⓓ 12 and $\frac{4}{5}$ cm long

38. Which decimal is shown by point A on the number line below?

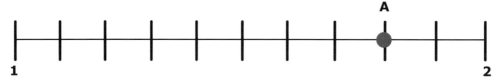

   Ⓐ 2.8
   Ⓑ 1.9
   Ⓒ 1.8
   Ⓓ 2.72

39. Homney Grill uses 9 pounds of beef to make 36 burgers.

   Part A. How many pounds of beef are in each burger? Show your work:

   Answer_____

   Part B. 12 friends came into the restaurant and bought the 36 burgers. How many burgers will each friend get? Show your work:

   Answer_____

40. Find the volume of this shape.

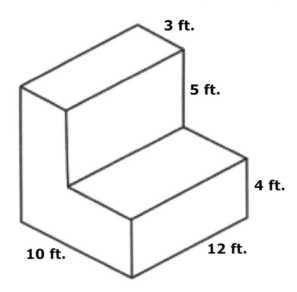

Volume:_____

Explain the steps you took to find the volume:

_____

_____

_____

_____

_____

41. Choose a fraction to complete the inequalities correctly.

Part A. 4/3 x _____ < 4/3   **Part B.** 12 x _____ < 12   **Part C.** 1/3 x _____ > 1/3

Part D. Explain how you know your answers are correct by choosing one problem to explain.

_____

_____

42. The table below shows the cost of a gym membership

Number of Classes (n)	Total Cost (c) (dollars)
8	$120
12	$180
16	$240
20	$300

Part A. Write an equation that describes the relationship between the number of classes (n) and the total cost (c).

_____

_____

Part B. Use the equation to find out how much 35 classes would cost: _____

43. Use the table to solve parts A and B below:

1. (4 x 6) + 46	A. Karen shared 46 gummy bears with her 6 friends and put the rest into 4 snack bags. How many gummy bears are in each snack bag?
2. 46 ÷ 7 = 6, r.4	B. Harry needs 46 nails for a project and buys 6 packs of 4 nails. How many more nails should he buy for the project?
3. 46 − (6 x 4)	C. Maggie babysat for 4 hours earning 6 dollars an hour. She combined her earnings with the 46 dollars she already had in the bank.

Part A. Match the expressions to the word problems. Write the letter of the word problem to match the equation on the line.

1. _____

2. _____

3. _____

Part B. Evaluate each expression:

1. _____

2. _____

3. _____

44. Draw and label an isosceles triangle in inches or centimeters.

    Explain how you can identify an isosceles triangle.

    _____

    _____

45. Solve Parts A and B below.

    Part A. The 5th grade class goes on a field trip to see a play. The cost for the bus ride to and from the play is $875. Each student ticket costs $12 and each adult ticket costs $14. If 89 students and 15 adults attend the play, what is the total cost of the field trip?

    Solve:

    _____

    _____

    Part B. The principal Mr. Jones finds out that he can receive a school discount and only has to pay $4/5$ of the original cost of the bus. After the discount, what does the school pay for the bus?

    _____

    _____

PRACTICE TEST ONE

NY STANDARDS ASSESSMENT

Mathematics Practice Test One Answer Key & Explanations

Mathematics Practice Test One
Answer Explanations

1. **B.** Point R is located at $3\,^2/_3$ from the origin zero. Each whole number is divided into thirds.
Difficulty Level: Easy
Standard: G.A.1

2. **C.** Follow the order of operations to solve: PEMDAS
31 + (14 − 2 x 3) x 2
31 + (14 − 6) x 2
31 + 8 x 2
31 + 16
Difficulty Level: Medium
Standard: OA.A.1

3. **C.** $^1/_3 + ^1/_6$
Use a common denominator of 6
$^1/_3 \times ^2/_2 = ^2/_6$
$^2/_6 + ^1/_6 = ^3/_6$
Difficulty Level: Easy
Standard: NF.A.1

4. **A.** $^1/_{100}$ is the same as dividing by 100. 4300 divide by 100 equals 43
Difficulty Level: Medium
Standard: NBT.A.1, NBT.B.7

5. **B.**
- Star and Circle. Coordinates: Star (3, 1); Circle (5, 9)
Difficulty Level: Difficult
Standard: G.A.1

6. **C.** 3 friends share 5 pizzas so divide the 5 pizzas between 3 people:
$5 \div 3 = 1$ and $^2/_3$
Each of the 5 pizzas are split into 3 equal parts, so each person will receive $^5/_3$ or 1 and $^2/_3$
Difficulty Level: Medium
Standard: NF.B.3

7. **A.** $0.6 \div 0.2 = 3$
The remaining lasagna is 0.6. Divide the lasagna into the 0.2 size pieces: $0.6 \div 0.2 = 3$, so she can make 3 pieces.
Difficulty Level: Medium
Standard: NBT.B.7

8. **D.** $^1/_{16}$ of her day is spent in each store. If half of her day is spent running errands at 8 stores for the same amount of time, divide $^1/_2 \div 8 = ^1/_2 \times ^1/_8 = ^1/_{16}$ of her day is spent in each store.
Difficulty Level: Medium
Standard: NF.B.7, NF.B.3

9. **D.** 4.823 —> 4,823
Numbers increase when multiplying by base 10. $10^3 = 1,000$
Difficulty Level: Medium
Standard: NBT.A.2, NBT.B.7

10. **A.** $4 \times ^2/_5$ = a number less than 4
Add $^2/_5 + ^2/_5 + ^2/_5 + ^2/_5 = ^8/_5$
$8 \div 5 = 1$ R 3 so $^8/_5 = 1$ and $^3/_5$, which is less than 4.
Difficulty Level: Medium
Standard: NF.B.4

11. **B.** $^1/_4$ of a foot = $^1/_4 \times 12$ inches (12 inches in 1 foot).
$1 \times 12 = 12$
$^{12}/_4 = 12 \div 4 = 3$ inches.
Difficulty Level: Easy
Standard: MD.A.1

12. **D.** First, find the volume of Kevin's prism: $6 \times 12 \times 8 = 576$ cubic inches. Carlos' prism is $^1/_3$ the volume of Kevin's prism so Carlos = $^1/_3$ of 576. To find $^1/_3$ of 576, multiply $576 \times ^1/_3 = (576 \times 1) \div 3 = 192$, so Carlos' prism has a volume of 192 cubic inches. Find the dimensions that equal 192 when multiplied: $6 \times 8 \times 4 = 192$
Difficulty Level: Medium
Standard: MD.C.5, NF.B.4

13. **B.** 168 cubic inches. The base layer is 6 cubes by 4 cubes so multiply to find the area of the base $6 \times 4 = 24$ cubes. The figure is 7 cubes tall so multiply the area of the base times the height of the box: $24 \times 7 = 168$ cubic inches.
Difficulty Level: Medium
Standard: MD.C.4

14. **D.** The total amount of miles covered was $^9/_{10}$ and $^1/_4$ of that he ran. Multiply $^1/_4 \times ^9/_{10}$ to find the part of the mile he ran.
Difficulty Level: Medium
Standard: NF.B.6

15. **C.** Volume of a rectangular prism = l x w x h
Difficulty Level: Easy
Standard: MD.C.5.B

16. **D.** The bottom layer consists of 10 cubes, the 2nd to bottom layer has 6, the 3rd layer from the bottom has 3 cubes and the top layer has 1 cube. Add all the cubes: $10 + 6 + 3 + 1 = 20$ cubic units.
Difficulty Level: Medium
Standard: MD.C.5

17. **A.** The rhombus and the square have 4 congruent sides – all sides the same length.
Difficulty Level: Easy
Standard: G.B.4

18. **A.** $1/4 \times 6 = 6/4$, add $1/4$ 6 times.
$1/4 + 1/4 + 1/4 + 1/4 + 1/4 + 1/4 = 6/4$
Difficulty Level: Easy
Standard: NF.B.5

19. **A.** Seventy-nine and 3 hundredths = 79.03
The other options have 70, 74, or 78 in the tens place so 79 is greater than those.
Difficulty Level: Medium
Standard: NBT.A.3

20. **A.** A rhombus is also a parallelogram because a parallelogram has opposite sides that are parallel and a rhombus fits this definition.

A square can be a rhombus because the definition of a rhombus is opposite sides parallel, and all sides congruent and a square fits these 2 characteristics.

A rectangle is also a quadrilateral because a quadrilateral has 4 sides and so does a rectangle.
Difficulty Level: Medium
Standard: G.B.3

21. **D.** x = 9, y = 32 (9, 32).
The pattern for x is x − 5 + 2
The pattern for y is y + 4 + 3
So subtract 5 to the x pattern and add 4 to the y pattern to get (9, 32).
Difficulty Level: Easy
Standard: OA.B.3

22. **C.** $[(7 \times 6) − 10] \div 4 = 8$
$[(7 \times 6) − 10] \div 4$
First find the number of cookies Marco made: 7 x 6. Then subtract 10 because he keeps 10 for himself $[(7 \times 6) − 10]$. Finally, divide by 4 because he shared 4 cookies with each friend.
Difficulty Level: Medium
Standard: OA.A.2, NBT.B.5, NBT.B.6

23. **B.** $4 \times 2/5$ or 4 groups of $2/5$ is the same as adding $2/5$ four times, which is shown in Choice B.
Difficulty Level: Easy
Standard: NF.B.4

24. **B.** 12 $1/2$ feet. 4 $1/7$ rounds to 4 because $1/7$ rounds to 0
3 $6/8$ rounds to 4 because $6/8$ rounds to 1 whole, it is greater than $1/2$
4 $4/9$ rounds to 4 $1/2$ because 4 is almost half of 9

Add 4 + 4 + 4 $1/2$ = 12 $1/2$ feet.
Difficulty Level: Medium
Standard: NF.A.2, NF.A.1

25. **B.** 58.63 rounds to 58.6 because 0.63 rounds to 0.6
Difficulty Level: Medium
Standard: NBT.A.4

26. **D.** 16 ounces in $1/3$ the bottle means add 16 + 16 + 16 to find how many ounces are in the whole bottle: 48 ounces.
48 ounces changed to cups:
8 ounces = 1 cup so divide 48 by 8 to find the number of cups in 48 ounces.
48 ÷ 8 = 6 cups.
Difficulty Level: Medium
Standard: MD.A.1

27. **A.** $6/8$ of the cookies are leftover and of the leftovers $1/4$ have nuts, so multiply $6/8 \times 3/4$ to find the remaining part without nuts.
$6/8 \times 3/4 = 18/32$ which can be reduced to $9/16$
Difficulty Level: Medium
Standard: NF.B.4

28. **A.** The base layer is 8 (2 x 4) cubes and the side flaps show the first row would be the side of the 1st layer and the 2nd row on the flap shows a 2nd layer: 8 + 8 = 16 cubes, so 16 cubes would fill the box.
Difficulty Level: Medium
Standard: MD.C.4

29. **C.** $1/16$ of the original water is in each glass. Samantha pours out $1/2$ of the water, and then $1/2$ of the remaining $1/2$, or $1/4$
$1/2$ is the same as $2/4$, so she has now poured out $2/4 + 1/4 = 3/4$ of the water.
Divide the remaining $1/4$ by 4, or $1/4 \div 4 = 1/4 \times 1/4$. This equals $1/16$
Difficulty Level: Difficult
Standard: NF.B.7, NF.A.1, NF.A.4

30. **B.** (5 x 25) − (4 x 20).
First find the total number of stickers he bought: 5 x 25
Then find the number of stickers he will give to all the students (4 stickers for 20 students = 4 x 20 = 80) Then subtract the number he has by the number he gives away: (5 x 25) − (4 x 20).
Difficulty Level: Medium
Standard: OA.A.1

31. **A.** Add the fractional amounts according to the number of ribbons for each length:

$1 + 1 + 1\frac{1}{4} + 1\frac{1}{4} + 1\frac{1}{4} + 1\frac{1}{2} + 1\frac{1}{2} + 1\frac{1}{2} + 1\frac{1}{2} + 1\frac{1}{2} + 1\frac{3}{4} + 1\frac{3}{4} + 1\frac{3}{4} + 2 + 2\frac{1}{4} + 2\frac{1}{4} = 25$ feet

$30\frac{1}{2} - 25 = 5\frac{1}{2}$ feet.

Difficulty Level: Medium
Standard: MD.A.2, NF.A.1

32. **B.** 58 inches. A square has 4 sides of equal length so divide the perimeter by 4 to find the length of each side: $232 \div 4 = 58$

Difficulty Level: Medium
Standard: G.B.4

33. **D.** Add $\frac{2}{8} + \frac{1}{3} + \frac{4}{6}$

Use a common denominator of 24:

$\frac{2}{8} \times \frac{3}{3} = \frac{6}{24}$
$\frac{1}{3} \times \frac{8}{8} = \frac{8}{24}$
$\frac{4}{6} \times \frac{4}{4} = \frac{16}{24}$

$\frac{6}{24} + \frac{8}{24} + \frac{16}{24} = \frac{30}{24} = 1$ and $\frac{6}{24}$

Then, add the whole numbers: $2 + 1 = 3$. Reduce $\frac{6}{24}$ by dividing by 6:

$\frac{6}{24} \div \frac{6}{6} = \frac{1}{4}$

Final answer: $4\frac{1}{4}$

Difficulty Level: Medium
Standard: NF.A.1

34. **B.** The polygon is a quadrilateral because it has 4 sides. It is a parallelogram because opposite sides are parallel and it's a polygon because it is a closed shape with no overlapping sides or curved edges.

Difficulty Level: Medium
Standard: G.B.3

35. **D.** The y-coordinate $3\frac{2}{3}$ is $2\frac{1}{3}$ units larger than the x-coordinate so the rule:

$x + 2\frac{1}{3} = y$ fits the ordered pairs $(1\frac{1}{3}, 3\frac{2}{3})$ and $(5, 7\frac{1}{3})$.

Difficulty Level: Difficult
Standard: G.A.2, NF.A.1

36. **A.** If the width is half of the height, take the height-6 and divide by 2 to find the width: $6 \div 2 = 3$ so the width is 3 inches.

Use the formula for volume to solve: $6 \times 3 \times n = 108$

$18 \times n = 108$, to find n, use division to solve: $108 \div 18 = 6$, so the missing height is 6 feet.

Difficulty Level: Medium
Standard: MD.C.5

37. **A.** 12 and $\frac{1}{7}$ cm long. $510 \div 42 = 12$ R 6. The remainder 6 centimeters can be split into 42 pieces which means each extra piece will be $\frac{6}{42} = \frac{6}{42} \div \frac{6}{6} = \frac{1}{7}$ so each piece will be $12\frac{1}{7}$ cm long.

Difficulty Level: Medium
Standard: NBT.B6

38. **C. 1.8.** Point A represents 1.8 because the point is past the whole number 1 and the number line is divided into ten equal pieces or tenths so the decimal is 1.8 or one and 8 tenths.

Difficulty Level: Easy
Standard: NBT.A.3

39. **Part A. $\frac{1}{4}$ pound.** If 9 pounds of beef is used to make 36 burgers, divide to find how much beef is in each burger: $9 \div 36 = \frac{9}{36}$ or $\frac{1}{4}$ pound is in each burger.

Part B. 3 burgers. If 12 friends want to share the 36 burgers, divide the 36 burgers by the 12 friends: $36 \div 12 = 3$ so they each take home 3 burgers.

Difficulty Level: Medium
Standard: NF.B.3

40. **660 cubic feet.** The large block on the bottom of the shape is 10 ft. by 12 ft. by 4 ft. so multiply the length x width x height to find the volume: $12 \times 10 \times 4 = 480$

Then the top block has a height of 5 ft. and a width of 3 ft. To find the length of the top rectangle, use the parallel length from the bottom rectangle, which is 12 feet. So multiply l x w x h = $5 \times 3 \times 12 = 180$. Finally, add the 2 volumes to find the combined volume of $480 + 180 = 660$ cubic feet.

Difficulty Level: Difficult
Standard: MD.C.5, NBT.B.5

41. **Part A. Any regular fraction will work here – not improper fraction or mixed number.**

Part B. Any regular fraction will work here – not improper fraction or mixed number.

Part C. The fraction must be an improper fraction in order to make the expression true.

Part D. Explanations will vary:

A fraction times an improper fraction = a fraction larger than the original fraction.

A whole number times a fraction equals a number smaller than the whole number factor.

An improper fraction (or mixed number) times a fraction equals a fraction smaller than the improper fraction.

Difficulty Level: Medium
Standard: NF.B.5

42. **Part A**. n x 15 = c

Part B. 35 classes costs $525. For example: 20 classes x 15 =$300.

Using the equation n x 15 = c, then 35 classes x 15 = $525

Difficulty Level: Medium
Standard: OA.B.3

---

43. **Part A.**
1. C
2. A
3. B

Part B. 1. $70

2. 1 gummy bear in each bag

3. 22 nails.

Karen shared 46 gummy bears with her 6 friends and put the rest into 4 snack bags- first 46 divided by 7 = 6 remainder 4, she divided the remaining 4 into 4 snack bags: 4 ÷ 4 = 1 in each bag.

Harry needs 46 nails for a project and buys 6 packs of 4 nails. How many more nails should he buy for the project? First multiply 6 x 4 = 24, subtract to find the number of nails he needs: 46 – 24 = 22

Maggie babysat for 4 hours earning 6 dollars an hour. She combined her earnings with the 46 dollars she already had in the bank. First multiply 6 x 4 = 24, then add it to the money she already has 46 + 24 = $70

Difficulty Level: Medium
Standard: OA.A.1

---

44. **Answers will vary.** Isosceles triangle has 2 opposite sides that are the same length.

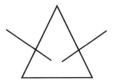

Difficulty Level: Medium
Standard: G.B.4

---

45. **Part A. $2,153 total for the adult and student tickets and bus.**

15 adults at $14 a ticket = 15 x 14 = 210

89 student tickets at $12 a ticket = 89 X 12 = 1,068

210 + 1068 = $1278 total for the adult & student tickets, then add the bus cost: 1278 + 875 = $2153

Part B. Cost of the bus after discount: $700. $4/5$ of 875 means multiply by $4/5$ to find the cost of the bus.

$4/5$ x 875 = 875 x 4 = 3500, 3500 ÷ 5 = 700 so the school will pay $700 after the discount, not $875

Difficulty Level: Difficult. Standard: NBT.B.5

Mathematics Practice Test Two Session One

1. The operation and the exponent are missing from the equation below.

$$23.4 \;\square\; 10^{\square} = 0.0234$$

   Choose the operation and the exponent that would make this equation true.
   - Ⓐ × and 3
   - Ⓑ ÷ and 2
   - ● ÷ and 3
   - Ⓓ × and 2

2. What is the least common denominator of $2/5$, $3/8$, and $1/2$?
   - ● 40
   - Ⓑ 10
   - Ⓒ 16
   - Ⓓ 80

3. How many more cubes are needed to fill this box completely with 1 cm cubes?

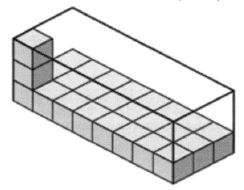

   - Ⓐ 42
   - Ⓑ 14
   - Ⓒ 72
   - ● 46

4. What part of this equation should be calculated third?

$$7 \times 4 - 4 + (12 - 3 \times 3) = n$$

   - ● 7 × 4
   - Ⓑ 4 − 4
   - Ⓒ 12 − 3
   - Ⓓ (12 − 3 × 3)

5. What is $1/100$ of 1.4?
   - Ⓐ 0.14
   - ● 0.014
   - Ⓒ 1.400
   - Ⓓ 140

6. A square and rhombus are shown below.

   Which attribute is true of one polygon but not the other polygon?
   - Ⓐ All sides are congruent.
   - Ⓑ Opposite sides are parallel.
   - ● All angles are right angles.
   - Ⓓ It is a quadrilateral.

7. What is another way to write the fraction $2/3$?
   - Ⓐ 2 x 3 =
   - Ⓑ 3 ÷ 2 =
   - Ⓒ 3 x 3 =
   - ● 2 ÷ 3 =

8. Which of these conversions are correct?
   - Ⓐ 800 mm = 8 cm
   - Ⓑ 8 m = 80 cm
   - ● 0.08 cm = 8 mm
   - Ⓓ 80 km = 80,000 mm

9. For an art project, Colby is dividing pieces of paper into fifths. How many fifth-sized pieces can Colby cut out of 6 pieces of paper?

   - Ⓐ 5
   - Ⓑ $1/5$
   - ● 30
   - Ⓓ 35

10. The juice bar makes 4,608 bottles of juice each month. They package the bottles into 72 cartons and deliver the cartons to 9 local supermarkets. How many bottles of juice does each supermarket receive?

   Ⓐ 8
   Ⓑ 64
   ● 512
   Ⓓ 71

11. There are 8 books on the shelf. This is $1/4$ of the total number of books in the classroom. What is the total number, n, of books in the classroom? Fill in the equation with the proper operation to solve this problem. (x, +, ÷, -)

$$8 \;\square\; 1/4 = n$$

   Ⓐ x
   Ⓑ +
   ● ÷
   Ⓓ -

12. Compare the expressions using one of the following <, >, =, +.

   4 twelves, tripled 5 times the difference of forty-two and nine

   ● <
   Ⓑ +
   Ⓒ >
   Ⓓ =

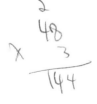

13. Jerry uses 15 cups of flour each week at his bakery. He uses 5 $2/5$ cup to make cookies and 6 $1/4$ cup to make the cakes. Then he uses 2 $2/10$ cup for pastries. How much flour does Jerry have left at the end of the week?

   Ⓐ He has 2 $1/7$ cup of flour remaining
   ● He has 1 $3/20$ cup of flour remaining
   Ⓒ He has 1 $1/6$ cup of flour remaining
   Ⓓ He has 13 $17/20$ cup of flour remaining

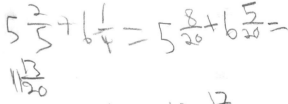

14. Cameron has 0.6 liters of soda. He has a measuring cup that holds 8 milliliters. He puts the soda in 22 different glasses by filling the measuring cup twice. How much soda does he use?
    - (A) 352 ml
    - (B) 16 ml
    - (C) 160 ml
    - (D) 1056 ml

15. Which equation can be used to find ¼ scaled up 6 times?
    - (A) ¼ × 6 =
    - (B) ¼ ÷ 6 =
    - (C) ¼ + 6 =
    - (D) ¼ + ¼ =

16. Use the coordinate grid to answer the question below.

    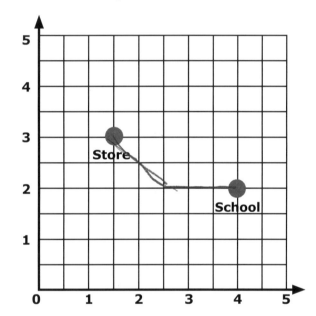

    How many units farther is the school than the store on the X –axis?
    - (A) 7
    - (B) 2
    - (C) 2.5
    - (D) 5

17. If a right triangle has one angle that measures 90°, what must be true about the other 2 angles?
    - (A) Each of the other 2 angles must be less than 90°
    - (B) The sum of the other 2 angles must be more than 90°
    - (C) The other 2 angles are obtuse angles
    - (D) The other 2 angles are right angles

PRACTICE TEST TWO

18. Which statement(s) below correctly describe(s) point M?

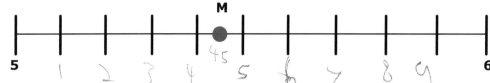

- (A) M < 5.2
- (B) M < 5.6
- (C) M = 5.5
- (D) M = 5.05

19. Which explanation is correct?
- (A) A square can be a rectangle because a square is a quadrilateral with 4 right angles.
- (B) A trapezoid is a parallelogram because opposite sides are parallel.
- (C) A rhombus is a square because a rhombus has 4 right angles.
- (D) Only some rhombuses are parallelograms.

20. Carin is using 3 feet of fabric to make 12 patches. What is the length of each patch in inches?
- (A) 3 inches
- (B) 1/4 inch
- (C) 4 inches
- (D) 1.5 inches

21. Amy, Hayden, and Sheryl share the gardening. Their garden is 20 feet long and they divide the gardening evenly. How should the the girls should divide up the garden?
- (A) 9 2/3 feet each
- (B) 6 1/3 feet each
- (C) 7 feet each
- (D) 6 2/3 feet each

22. Sue writes a number pattern that starts at 28, subtracts 5 and adds 2 as the rule. Calvin writes a number pattern that starts at 33, adds 2 and then subtracts 4 as the rule. What is the fifth term in both patterns?
- (A) (15, 20)
- (B) (18, 22)
- (C) (16, 25)
- (D) (22, 29)

23. Karl has ⁵/₈ of a pizza leftover from his dinner. Of the leftover pizza, ¹/₃ of it has pepperoni. What fraction of the entire pizza is leftover with pepperoni?
   - Ⓐ ⁷/₂₄
   - Ⓑ ²/₅
   - Ⓒ ²/₃
   - ● ⁵/₂₄

24. What is this number in standard form?

$$(50 \times 10^3) + (0.3 \times 10^2) + (7 \times \tfrac{1}{100}) + (66 \times \tfrac{1}{1000})$$

   - Ⓐ 50,090.123
   - Ⓑ 500,030.136
   - Ⓒ 5,030.136
   - Ⓓ 50,030.136

25. Carol's rectangle measures ¹/₄ foot long and ³/₆ foot wide. What is the area of the box?
   - Ⓐ ⁴/₁₀ sq. feet
   - Ⓑ ¹/₈ sq. feet
   - Ⓒ ²/₅ sq. feet
   - Ⓓ ²/₄ sq. feet

26. Six elk weigh ³/₄ of a ton. How much does each elk weigh in pounds?
   - Ⓐ 200 pounds
   - Ⓑ 300 pounds
   - Ⓒ 350 pounds
   - Ⓓ 250 pounds

27. Which pair of decimals correctly rounds 34.48 to two different place values?
   - Ⓐ 34.40 and 35.0
   - Ⓑ 34.5 and 34.0
   - Ⓒ 34.50 and 35.0
   - Ⓓ 34.5 and 34.8

28. A rectangular prism has a volume of 624 cubic centimeters. The length is 12 centimeters and a width of 4 centimeters. What is the height of the prism?
   - Ⓐ 14 centimeters
   - Ⓑ 12 centimeters
   - Ⓒ 13 centimeters
   - Ⓓ 16 centimeters

PRACTICE TEST TWO

29. Solve:

$$\tfrac{3}{4} + \tfrac{1}{3} - \tfrac{1}{6} =$$

Ⓐ $\tfrac{11}{12}$

Ⓑ $\tfrac{13}{12}$

Ⓒ $\tfrac{3}{1}$

Ⓓ 1 and $\tfrac{1}{6}$

30. The table below shows the layers and number of centimeter cubes in rectangular prisms.

Prism	Number of Layers	Number of Cubes in Each Layer
Prism H	5	6
Prism Y	3	8
Prism J	6	4
Prism R	7	5

Which prism has the greatest volume?
Ⓐ Prism H
Ⓑ Prism Y
Ⓒ Prism J
Ⓓ Prism R

Session Two

31. What is the volume of this figure in cubic units?

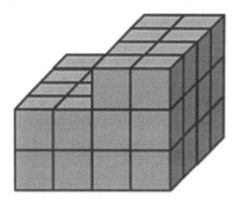

- Ⓐ 40 cubic units
- Ⓑ 32 cubic units
- Ⓒ 42 cubic units
- Ⓓ 36 cubit units

32. Which phrase describes the volume of a figure with dimensions of 4 units by 5 units by 2 units?
- Ⓐ A figure that can be covered with 40 cubes each measuring 1 square unit.
- Ⓑ A figure that can be filled with 40 cubes each measuring 1 cubic unit.
- Ⓒ A figure that can be filled with 1 cube measuring 40 units on each edge.
- Ⓓ A figure that can be covered with 1 square that measures 40 units on each edge.

33. The students in Ms. Macey's class took a survey. Each student voted for their favorite pet out of 3 choices: dog, cat, bird.

- $2/9$ of the students voted for dogs
- $4/6$ of the students voted for cats

What fraction of the number of students voted for birds?

- Ⓐ $16/18$
- Ⓑ $2/9$
- Ⓒ $2/6$
- Ⓓ $1/9$

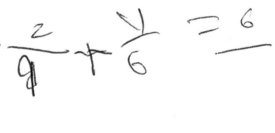

34. Which decimal below is the smallest?
- Ⓐ $2.81 \div 10^3$
- Ⓑ $2.8 \div 100$
- Ⓒ $28.4 \times 1/10$
- Ⓓ $2.89 \times 1/100$

35. Carrie and her 5 friends are volunteering to organize the food pantry. They will sort and organize 4 boxes of food. How much will each girl have to organize?
    A) 4/5 of a box
    B) 6/4 of a box
    C) 2/3 of a box
    D) 1/2 of a box

36. Which polygon has 2 sets of opposite angles that are equivalent?
    A) pentagon
    B) trapezoid
    C) rhombus
    D) isosceles triangle

37. Jaime is measuring a dresser in his house. The area of the base of the dresser is 352 square inches and the height is 48 inches. What is the volume of the dresser?
    A) 16,746 cubic inches
    B) 16,896 cubic inches
    C) 16,596 cubic inches
    D) 16,886 cubic inches

38. The table below shows a set of numbers.

A	B
78.987	0.078987
5682.3	5.6823
409.6	0.4096

Which rule can be used to explain the relationship between column A and column B? Select all that apply.
    A) A × 10³ = B
    B) A ÷ 10³ = B
    C) B × 1/1000 = A
    D) A × 1/100 = B

39. Carlos' doctor told him to drink 8 ounces of water 8 times a day. He has a water bottle that holds 1 1/2 pints. Carlos fills up his water bottle 3 times a day and drinks the entire thing.

Part A. Use the number line to show how much water Carlos is drinking in pints by using arrow jumps to show each water bottle consumed.

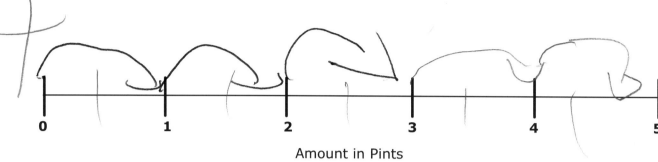

Amount in Pints

Part B. Is Carlos drinking enough water? Explain your reasoning.

___

40. Mrs. Bartley is organizing her kitchen. Her large container holds 10 2/3 cups of baking items. Her medium sized container holds 3/4 of the larger container. Her smallest container holds 3/4 of the medium-sized container. What is the total amount of storage space in cups that Mrs. Bartley can store in the containers?

Show your work:

Answer: 10 27/12

41. The line plot shows the amount of string Sarah used to make jewelry. She cut the pieces into the sizes shown below.

```
                          X
                    X     X
                    X     X
                    X     X     X
                    X     X     X     X
         +----+-----+-----+-----+-----+----
         0   ¼     ½     ¾     1
              Amount of String in Feet
```

Part A. How many inches of string did Sarah use to make the 2 pieces that are ¾ foot in length?

Answer: _____

Part B. Sarah had 1 foot of string left over after cutting the pieces. How much string did Sarah have to start?

Answer: _____

42. Mrs. Bee is packing up the books in her classroom.
   • The box she is using to hold her books is 12 inches long, 10 inches wide, and 18 inches tall.
   • Each book has the same dimensions of 10 inches tall, 4 inches wide, and 2 inches in height.
   • How many books can she fit into the box if there is no overlapping or unused space?
   Show your work:

Answer: _____

43. Sam and Carly work at the bakery and start saving their money. Sam starts by saving $12 the first week and each week after that he adds $3 to his weekly savings. Carly saves $15 the first week and adds $2 to her savings each week. Complete the table to show the kids' total savings at the end of each week for the first 5 weeks.

Week	1	2	3	4	5
Sam's Savings					
Carly's Savings					

How much money will Sam and Carly have after 10 weeks of savings?

Answer: _____

44. Use the figure below to answer the questions:

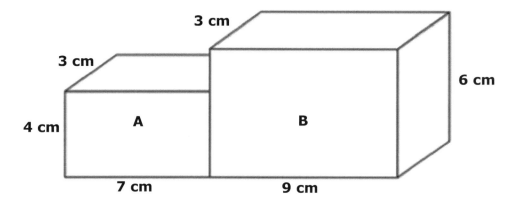

What is the volume of prism A? _____

What is the volume of prism B? _____

What is the volume of the entire figure? _____

45. Brendan ran ⁵/₈ of a mile on Saturday and ran ¹/₄ of a mile on Sunday. Brendan said he ran a total of ¹/₂ mile because ⁵/₈ + ¹/₄ = ⁶/₁₂ which equals ¹/₂.

A. Explain why his reasoning is incorrect using the number line.

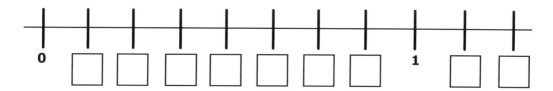

B. What is the total amount of miles Brendan ran on Saturday and Sunday?

Mathematics Practice Test Two Answer Key & Explanations

Mathematics Practice Test Two
Answer Explanations

1. **C.** $10^3 = 1000$ and $23.4 \div 1000 = 0.234$
Difficulty Level: Medium
Standard: NBT.A.2

2. **A.** 40. The denominators of 5, 8 and 2 have 40 as their least common multiple:

5, 10, 15, 20, 25, 30, 35, 40

8, 16, 24, 32, 40
Difficulty Level: Easy
Standard: NF.A.1

3. **D.** 46 cubes are needed to fill the box. First, find the volume of the box by multiplying length x width x height = 3 x 8 x 3 = 72 cubic cm.

Then, subtract the visible cubes from the total volume to find the amount of cubes needed to fill the box. There are 26 cubes shown, subtract 72 – 26 = 46 cubes are needed to fill the box.
Difficulty Level: Medium
Standard: MD.C.4, MD.C.5

4. **A.** 7 x 4. In this equation: 7 x 4 – 4 + (12 – 3 x 3)

The expression in the parenthesis must be completed first: (12 – 3 x 3) First complete 3 x 3 = 9, then subtract 12 – 9 = 3 as the second step following the order of operations PEDMAS.

The remaining equation is 7 x 4 – 4 + 3

The third step is 7 x 4, following the order of operations PEDMAS.
Difficulty Level: Easy
Standard: OA.A.1

5. **B.** $1/100$ is the same as dividing by 100. 1.4 divided by 100 is moving 2 decimal places to left = 0.014
Difficulty Level: Easy
Standard: NBT.A.1

6. **C.** The square does have all right angles and a rhombus does not.
Difficulty Level: Medium
Standard: G.B.3

7. **D.** $2/3$ can be written as 2 ÷ 3 as a division equation because 2 pizzas shared with 3 people would show each person getting $2/3$ of the pizza.
Difficulty Level: Easy
Standard: NF.B.3

8. **D.** 80 km = 80,000 m because there are 1000 m in 1 km so multiply 80 km x 1000 = 80,000 meters in 80 km.

The others are incorrect. 80 mm = 8 cm because 1 cm equals 10 mm so 8 cm x 10 = 80 mm.

0.8cm = 8 mm

There are 10 mm in 1 cm so multiply 0.8 x 10 to find the number of mm in 0.8 cm, 0.8 x 10 = 8 mm
Difficulty Level: Medium
Standard: MD.A.1

9. **C.** 30 pieces of paper. 6 pieces of paper cut into $1/5$ sized pieces is $6 \div 1/5 = 6 \times 5 = 30$ pieces of paper.
Difficulty Level: Easy
Standard: NF.B.7, NF.B.3

10. **C.** 512 bottles of juice. 4608 bottles divided into 72 cartons means 4608 ÷ 72 = 64 bottles in a carton.

72 cartons divided by 9 stores = 72 ÷ 9 = 8 cartons per each store.

If each store receives 8 cartons and there are 64 bottles in each carton, multiply to find the number of bottles each store receives: 8 x 64 = 512 bottles.
Difficulty Level: Difficult
Standard: NBT.A.6, NBT.A.5

11. **C.** 8 books on the shelf comprise $1/4$ of all the books.

$8 \div 1/4 = 8 \times 4 = 32$, there are 32 books total in the classroom.
Difficulty Level: Medium
Standard: NF.B.7, NF.B.3

12. **A.** <. 4 twelves is the same has saying 4 group of 12 which equals 4 x 12 = 48 and 3 x 48 =144

5 times the difference of forty-two and nine is 5 x (42-9)

42 – 9 = 33

5 x 33 = 165

144 < 165
Difficulty Level: Medium
Standard: OA.A.2

13. **B.** He has 1 $3/20$ cup of flour remaining. The first step is to change the fractions to have a common denominator of 20.

First, find a common denominator for 5, 4, and 10 which is 20

Find equivalent fractions of each using the denominator of 20:

$2/5 \times 4/4 = 8/20$

$1/4 \times 5/5 = 5/20$

$2/10 \times 2/2 = 4/20$

Then add the whole numbers: $5 + 6 + 2 = 13$

Add the fractions: $8/20 + 5/20 + 4/20 = 17/20$ so Jerry used 13 and $17/20$ cups of flour.

To find the remaining four, subtract $15 - 13$ and $17/20$

Convert 15 into 14 and $20/20$ to subtract:

$14 - 13 = 1$

$20/20 - 17/20 = 3/20$

so he has 1 and $3/20$ cup of flour remaining.

Difficulty Level: Difficult
Standard: NF.A.2, NF.A.1

14. **A.** 352 ml Cameron pours 2 measuring cups of 8 milliliters so multiply $8 \times 2 = 16$ milliliters in each glass. He fill 22 glasses so multiply $16 \times 22 = 352$ milliliters.

Difficulty Level: Medium
Standard: MD.A.1, NBT.B.4, NBT.B.5

15. **A.** $1/4$ scaled up 6 times is the same as multiplying $1/4 \times 6$ or adding $1/4$ 6 times.

Difficulty Level: Easy
Standard: NF.B.5

16. **C.** 2 $1/2$ units. The school is located at 4 on the X-axis and the store is located at 1 $1/2$ on the X-axis. Subtract to find the difference: $4 - 1\ 1/2 = 2\ 1/2$

Difficulty Level: Medium
Standard: G.A.1, N.F.1

17. **A.** The sum of the interior angles in a triangle equals 180 degrees so a right triangle has one angle that is 90° and the other 2 angles must be less than 90° to equal a total of 180 degrees.

Difficulty Level: Easy
Standard: G.B.3

18. **B.** M < 5.6 This comparison is true because M is located at 5.45 and 5.45 < 5.6

Difficulty Level: Easy
Standard: NBT.A.3

19. **A.** A square can be a rectangle because a square is a quadrilateral with 4 right angles. But a rectangle cannot be a square because a square must have 4 congruent sides and rectangles do not have all sides the same length.

Difficulty Level: Medium
Standard: G.A.4

20. **A.** 3 inches.

3 feet of fabric divided into 12 patches = $3 \div 12 = 3/12$ or $1/4$ of a foot.

$1/4$ of a foot in inches means multiply $1/4 \times 12$ since there are 12 inches in 1 foot. $1/4 \times 12 = 12/4 = 3$ inches.

Difficulty Level: Medium
Standard: NF.B.3, NF.B.4

21. **D.** 6 $2/3$ feet. $20 \div 3 = 6$ R 2 which means each girl will work on 6 and $2/3$ feet of the garden.

Difficulty Level: Medium
Standard: NF.B.3

22. **D.** Start at 28: minus 5, then add 2:

28, 23, 25, 20, <u>22</u>

Start at 33: add 2 then subtract 4:

33, 35, 31, 33, <u>29</u>

So the fifth term in each pattern is (22, 29)

Difficulty Level: Medium
Standard: OA.B.3

23. **D.** $5/24$. $5/8 \times 1/3 = 5/24$, so $5/24$ of the entire pizza is leftover with pepperoni.

Difficulty Level: Medium
Standard: NF.B.4

24. **D.** 50,030.136. $(50 \times 10^3) + (0.3 \times 10^2) + (7 \times 1/100) + (66 \times 1/1000)$

$10^3 = 10 \times 10 \times 10 = 1000$

$50 \times 1000 = 50,000$

$10^2 = 10 \times 10 = 100$

$0.3 \times 100 = 30$

$7 \times 1/100 = 7 \times 0.01 = 0.07$

$66 \times 1/1000 = 66 \times 0.001 = 0.066$

Add up the products: $50,000 + 30 + 0.07 + 0.066 = 50,030.136$

Difficulty Level: Medium
Standard: NBT.A.2

25. **B.** $1/4 \times 3/6 = 3/24$ which can be reduced to $1/8$

$3 \div 3 = 1$

$24 \div 3 = 8 = 1/8$ square feet.

Difficulty Level: NF.B.4b
Standard: Easy

26. **D.** $3/4$ of a ton means multiply $3/4$ by a ton.

1 ton = 2000 pounds

$3/4 \times 2000 = 3 \times 2000 = 6000$

$6000 \div 4 = 1500$ pounds

If 6 elk weighed 1500 pounds, divide to find the weight of each.

1500 ÷ 6 = 250 pounds each.

Difficulty Level: Medium
Standard: MD.A.1, NF.B.4

27. **B.** 34.48 rounds to 34.5 because the 8 in the hundredths place moves the tenths place to 5 = 34.5

34.48 rounds to 34.0 in the ones place because the 4 tenths does not change the ones place.

Difficulty Level: Easy
Standard: NBT.A.4

28. **C.** Volume = l x w x h. The length and width are already known: 12 x 4 = 48

48 x h = 624

Divide to find the height:

624 ÷ 48 = 13

Difficulty Level: Medium
Standard: MD.C.5

29. **A.** $^{11}/_{12}$. Use a common denominator of 12 to solve:

$^{3}/_{4}$ x $^{3}/_{3}$ = $^{9}/_{12}$

$^{1}/_{3}$ x $^{4}/_{4}$ = $^{4}/_{12}$

Add $^{9}/_{12}$ + $^{4}/_{12}$ = $^{13}/_{12}$

Subtract $^{13}/_{12}$ – $^{1}/_{6}$ =

$^{1}/_{6}$ x $^{2}/_{2}$ = $^{2}/_{12}$

$^{13}/_{12}$ – $^{2}/_{12}$ = $^{11}/_{12}$

Difficulty Level: Easy
Standard: NF.A.1

30. **D.** Prism R has the largest volume because 7 layers with 5 cubes in each layer – 7 x 5 = 35

Volume – l x w x h or area x height. In this case, we know the area- the number of cubes in each layer, so multiply 5 x7 to find the volume.

Difficulty Level: Medium
Standard: MD.C.5

31. **A.** The bottom section is 4 units long by 4 units wide and 2 units tall – find the volume 4 x 4 x 2 = 32

The top section is 2 units wide by 4 units long by 1 unit tall. Find the volume 1 x 4 x 2 = 8

Add the volumes: 32 + 8 = 40 units.

Difficulty Level: Easy
Standard: MD.C.4, MD.C.5

32. **B.** A figure that can be filled with 40 cubes each measuring 1 cubic unit explains the figure because to find the volume, multiply 4 x 5 x 2 = 40 cubic units.

Volume is the measurement of capacity and the figure can be filled with 40 cubic units.

Difficulty Level: Medium
Standard: MD.C.3

33. **D.** First, use a common denominator of 18 to find the total amount of students that voted for cats and dogs:

$^{2}/_{9}$ + $^{4}/_{6}$

$^{2}/_{9}$ x $^{2}/_{2}$ = $^{4}/_{18}$

$^{4}/_{6}$ x $^{3}/_{3}$ = $^{12}/_{18}$

$^{4}/_{18}$ + $^{12}/_{18}$ = $^{16}/_{18}$

To find the remaining students that voted for birds subtract $^{18}/_{18}$ (the total amount of students) – $^{16}/_{18}$ = $^{2}/_{18}$

$^{2}/_{18}$ can be simplified to $^{1}/_{9}$ because 2 ÷ 2 – 1

18 ÷ 2 = 9 = $^{1}/_{9}$ of the students chose birds.

Difficulty Level: Medium
Standard: NF.A.1, NF.A.2

34. **A.** 2.81 ÷ 10^3

10^3 = 10 x 10 x 10 = 1000

2.81 ÷ 1000 = 0.00281 which is the smallest decimal listed.

Difficulty Level: Medium
Standard: NBT.A.3

35. **C.** Four boxes divided between 6 total people (Carrie plus 5 friends) should be 4 divided by 6 or $^{4}/_{6}$ = $^{2}/_{3}$

Difficulty Level: Medium
Standard: NF.B.3

36. **C.** A rhombus has 2 sets of opposite angles that are the same measure.

Difficulty Level: Easy
Standard: G.B.4

37. **B.** To find the volume, multiply the area of the base x the height = 352 x 48 = 16,896 cubic inches.

Difficulty Level: Medium
Standard: MD.C.5

38. **B.** Each value in the B column is the value in the A column divided by 1000, or A ÷ 10^3 (1000 = 10^3).

Difficulty Level: Medium
Standard: NBT.A.2, NBT.B.3

39. **See explanation and number line.** 8 ounces 8 times a day means multiply to find the total

number of ounces Carlos needs to drink each day = 8 x 8 = 64 oz.

1 $\frac{1}{2}$ pints 3 times a day means multiply 1 $\frac{1}{2}$ x 3 = 4 $\frac{1}{2}$ pints each day.

Convert the number of pints to ounces by multiply by 16 since there are 16 ounces in 1 pint.

4 $\frac{1}{2}$ x 16

Change 4 $\frac{1}{2}$ to an improper fraction:
$\frac{9}{2}$ x 16 = 9 x 16 = 144 ÷ 2 = 72.

72 > 64 so YES Carlos is drinking enough water each day.

Difficulty Level: Difficult
Standard: MD.A.1, NBT.B.5, NBT.B.6

40. **Large: 10 $\frac{2}{3}$ cup**

Medium: 8 cups

Small: 6 cups

24 and $\frac{2}{3}$ cups. If the largest container holds 10 and $\frac{2}{3}$ cups and the medium container is $\frac{3}{4}$ of that, them multiply to find the size of the medium container.

10 and $\frac{2}{3}$ x $\frac{3}{4}$

Convert 10 $\frac{2}{3}$ into a mixed number: 10 x 3 = 30 + 3 = 32

$\frac{32}{3}$ x $\frac{3}{4}$ = $\frac{96}{12}$ and 96 ÷ 12 = 8 so the medium container holds 8 cups.

The smallest container is $\frac{3}{4}$ of the medium container, 8 so $\frac{3}{4}$ of 8 = $\frac{3}{4}$ x 8 = 3 x 8 = 24

$\frac{24}{4}$ = 24 ÷ 4 = 6 so the smallest container holds 6 cups.

Add the amount each container can hold to find the total amount of storage in cups: 10 and $\frac{2}{3}$ + 8 + 6 = 24 and $\frac{2}{3}$ cups.

Difficulty Level: Medium
Standard: NF.B.6

41. **Part A. 18 inches   Part B. 6 $\frac{1}{4}$ feet of string total.**

Part A. Add $\frac{3}{4}$ + $\frac{3}{4}$ to find the number of feet used to make both pieces = $\frac{6}{4}$ = 1 and $\frac{2}{4}$ feet or 1 $\frac{1}{2}$ feet. Convert 1 $\frac{1}{2}$ feet into inches: 1 foot = 12 inches. $\frac{1}{2}$ foot = 6 inches so she used 18 inches to make the $\frac{3}{4}$ foot sized pieces.

Part B. Add all the pieces together to find the total amount of string used to make the pieces:

$\frac{1}{4}$ + $\frac{1}{4}$ + $\frac{1}{4}$ = $\frac{3}{4}$
$\frac{1}{2}$ + $\frac{1}{2}$ + $\frac{1}{2}$ + $\frac{1}{2}$ = 2
$\frac{3}{4}$ + $\frac{3}{4}$ = $\frac{6}{4}$ or 1 $\frac{1}{2}$

Add up the totals: $\frac{3}{4}$ + 2 + 1 $\frac{1}{2}$ = 4 $\frac{1}{4}$ feet.

Add the 1 piece of 1 foot string plus the 1 foot she had leftover = 6 $\frac{1}{4}$ feet of string total.

Difficulty Level: Difficult
Standard: MD.B.2, NF.B.4

42. **The box can hold 27 books.** First, find the volume of the box: 12 x 10 x 18 = 2160 cubic inches.

Find the volume of each book: 10 x 4 x 2 = 80 cubic inches. Divide the total volume available- the box – 2160 by the space each book will take up – 80

2160 ÷ 80 = 27 books.

The box can hold 27 books.

Difficulty Level: Difficult
Standard: MD.C.5, NBT.B.4, NBT.B.5

43. **Sam: 12, 15, 18, 21, 24**

Carly: 15, 17, 19, 21, 23

After 10 weeks they will have $72. Sam: 12 + 3 = 15 + 3 = 18 + 3 = 21 + 3 = 24

Carly: 15 + 2 = 17 + 2 = 19 + 2 = 21 + 2 = 23

After 10 weeks, Sam will have 24 plus 5 x 3, so he will have 24 + 15 = $39

After 10 weeks, Carly will have 23 + 5 x 2, so she will have 23 + 10 = $33

39 + 33 = $72

Difficulty Level: Medium
Standard: OA.B.3

44. **Part A. 84 cubic cm**

Part B. 162 cubic cm

Part C. 246 cubic cm

The dimensions of prism A are 3 x 4 x 7 = 84 cubic cm. The dimensions of prism B are 9 x 6 x 3 = 162 cubic cm. Add to find the total volume: 162 + 84 = 246 cubic cm.

Difficulty Level: Medium
Standard: NBT.A.4

45. **Parts A and B:** Brendan is incorrect because $\frac{5}{8}$ is more than $\frac{1}{2}$ so he could not have run $\frac{1}{2}$ miles total.

$\frac{1}{4}$ = $\frac{1}{4}$ x $\frac{2}{2}$ = $\frac{2}{8}$

$\frac{5}{8}$ + $\frac{2}{8}$ = $\frac{7}{8}$ miles total.

Difficulty Level: Medium
Standard: NF.A.2

Made in the USA
Middletown, DE
06 November 2021